Mount Holly

New Jersey

Mount Holly

New Jersey

A Hometown Reinvented

Dennis C. Rizzo

The History Press

Published by The History Press
Charleston, SC 29403
www.historypress.net

Front and back cover images: Turn-of-the-century Mount Holly was a quieter place. The front shows Mill Street circa the late 1800s; the back provides a glimpse of High Street, also during that time. The two streets intersect near the Mill Dam Park, right alongside the Rancocas Creek, in the heart of Mount Holly. *Both photos courtesy of the Mount Holly Historical Society.*

Back cover inset: John Sellers's 1677 map of New Jersey captured the colony during a particularly tumultous time in its history. The British seized the territory from the Dutch in 1664, only to see the Dutch recapture it in 1673. Following the 1674 Treaty of Westminster, which ceded the land back to the English, the colony was partitioned into East and West Jersey…all of which must have greatly frustrated Sellers's efforts at rendering the region accurately. *Map courtesy of the New Jersey State Archives (Trenton).*

First published 2007

Manufactured in the United States

ISBN 978.1.59629.276.5

Library of Congress CIP data applied for.

Notice: The information in this book is true and complete to the best of our knowledge. It is offered without guarantee on the part of the author or The History Press. The author and The History Press disclaim all liability in connection with the use of this book.

To Michael B., Ariana M. and Zoe C.—the future.

Contents

Foreword, by Karl Mehl 9

Preface 11

1. The Common People: Lenape 15
2. Evolution of Place 23
3. Friends and Neighbors 43
4. The Place Builds a Reputation 59
5. The Battle of Mount Holly: Rebellion and Aftermath 72
6. Political, Economic and Agricultural Leadership 87
7. A Wound That Will Not Heal 103
8. The Gilded Age: Gardens and Debutantes 110
9. The Doughboys Arrive—And Stay 129
10. Decline and Rebirth 142

Notes 149

Bibliography 155

Foreword

The Merriam-Webster dictionary defines history as a chronological record of significant events often with an explanation of their causes. It continues on to say history is a branch of knowledge that records and explains past events. A good news reporter works hard to convey the facts about what happened, where it happened, how it happened and when it happened—with a possible explanation of why it happened.

Unfortunately, many reporters of history, using the above writing style, often produce dry and uninteresting tomes. You, like I, have probably read such books or stories throughout our school years. And you, as well as I, have learned to dislike the study of history as a result of that. But the question still remains, "Is learning about history important?"

In today's technologically enriched age, most would say no. I beg to differ.

Over the years I have learned that by knowing what has happened in the past, I can avoid the same downfalls experienced by my ancestors and thus succeed in my endeavors. From each of us to the massiveness of the federal governments across the world, the historical past gives us clues to the future. My mother used to say, "You must learn from your mistakes." Another often heard phrase is "those who ignore history are doomed to repeat it." Think about these two phrases as you read this book.

Dennis Rizzo has an abiding interest in the history of our area, our town and our country. He goes one step further than the definition of the historical writer outlined above. He adds the human touch to his reporting so you can imagine yourself being part of the historical scene, not just an outsider reading about it. Throughout his writing you get to see the successes and failures of the people at that time. We learn by analyzing these points to ensure that negative actions shall never be repeated in the future.

Karl Mehl

Preface

In writing, like in any other creative sport, you have rules and regulations on how and why to perform certain actions. But the writer controls what those actions are—it's called creative license. I like creative license, and so do my children. Creative license means you can invent things. You can say, with a straight face, that "Bear-Bear" can fly when he clearly is not airworthy. You can kill off a character, then revise and bring her back if the story calls for it—except with history.

Once characters in history are killed off they're pretty much out of the story. Yes, there are estates, family squabbles, rivalries and all that, but once history passes you by that's about all there is to it. It puts a damper on creative license.

Much local history relates the stories of individuals, weaving in information about the times to add color and flavor and put their lives in perspective. However, telling history based solely on individuals can become a litany of "begats," in the style of Genesis. It can be interesting to the homeowner searching for a legacy to his house, but dry as an old bone in my dog's dish to the average reader. Unless, of course, you decide to try to write a history with a little creative license.

Preparing a history seemed like it would be a challenge and fun. I had been involved in the local history association, shown my restored homes on the candlelight tour a couple of times and participated in various phases of the downtown revitalization effort as one of a hundred volunteers. I prepared an event from scratch (Iron Works Hill commemoration) with a good friend, Ian Johns. I edited the local newsletter, trying to blend some humor with direct information. In doing this I had read much of what was extant about Mount Holly—at times in detail so excruciating I looked for someone who could make it endurable. But I'm fascinated with history.

So, what would it take to write something on my own?

Don't ask. Or, if you do, ask my wife, Elizabeth van Houtte, not me. She knows the truth. I only know what went on inside my head for several months as this story of our adopted hometown evolved.

From the time the publishers announced an interest in New Jersey history for The History Press, to the time I submitted the manuscript, Elizabeth supported my insanity with cool and calm. I discovered that the historian can get distracted easily by threads of information that lead to more threads of information, etc., until he or she is so far off topic as to require a complete rewrite. Elizabeth pulled me back from the edge of disaster several times.

She helped me accept that, even with the Internet at my fingertips (literally), I could never do justice to the detail and research completed by Henry Shinn in his 1957 tome on Mount Holly. I didn't have the local perspective of Zachariah Read, whose 1859 detailed chronology and listing of prominent townspeople has served as a guidebook for over 150 years. The letters and manuscripts and interviews these people (and others) went through could not be recaptured in the few months I had. In the end I discovered that they should not be reworked, but simply applied and relied on.

Oxymoron comes to mind when someone asks what history is to the average person; how we always seem to think that either our times are the "best" times, or "the good old days" were better than today. "Kids these days…" (you can fill in the blank). We rarely imagine the father in ancient Rome complaining to his barber about his son's insolence or daughter's wastefulness. What of the French peasant whose son was drafted to join Napoleon's army? Was he upset or resigned or happy not to have one more mouth to feed? Did they have boot camp graduation like we do? If so, was there beer?

It is this type of nonlinear thinking that has always gotten me into trouble. These scenarios might seem destined for comic theater, but I'd bet they're pretty close to the truth. An early writing instructor of mine once told the class that writers needed to exercise their imaginations. I was set; I've been accused of daydreaming my whole life. With writing at least I can do it with less social derision.

And so, this book on Mount Holly. Without Elizabeth's understanding and patience it never would have happened. She's working on her dissertation and set it aside so I could write (*mmmpppfff*). Ariana Marie and Zoë Claire wisely stayed clear (much thanks to Julia Schnelle for that) but provided much needed R&R from time to time. Mike Rizzo offered his *condolences* (which means "good luck," I suppose), and Grandpa Victor provided encouragement. But, as they say in Ginsu Knife Land, "That's not all."

The History Press opened their doors and let a first-timer in. Saunders Robinson put up with my anxiety and got this project through.

Eleanor Rich, Gladys Danser and the entire Mount Holly Historical Society opened their hearts, and their archives, to me. My only regret is we could not get at the individual stories and details I know are there. That's our next effort. And J.C. Cowgill, wherever you are—thanks.

Alicia McShulkis was a critical companion via the Internet on those late working evenings when I had a detail that needed quick corroboration, or needed to scream into the early morning air. Karl Mehl has been a mentor in this and other projects, and believes in this writer (even when I don't believe in myself).

Alicia, Rocky D'Entrement, Larry Tigar and Heidi Winzinger helped locate the thousands of illustrations and photographs from which those in here were culled. Mike Eck of the Mount Holly Library and Lyceum and Paula Manzella of the Burlington County Library System helped navigate interlibrary loans and locked repositories, locate remote resources and find one-of-a-kind manuscripts. The staff of the New Jersey State Archives were immensely helpful, especially Joanne Nestor, the staff photographer, with whose skill we were able to get the 1677 John Sellers map into print.

And to Jed Rizzo and Chloe "the Bean" van Houtte—our loyal and loving Cocker Spaniels—when it's on the desk it's *my* sandwich.

1.

The Common People

Lenape

The small deerskin orb floated through still spring air, unusually cool for this time of year. Tired and bruised from hours of persuasion to move in one direction or another, it came to rest on a tuft of grass lining the creek called Ankokus. It had but a moment's peace before being kicked again, this time into the hands of a young woman. Holding her hair from in front of her eyes with one hand and grasping the ball tightly in the other, the woman ran as fast as she could to the line marked on the edge of the meadow. With a grunt and last gasp of air, her husband grabbing at the hem of her doeskin dress, she dove across the goal. An old woman watching from nearby placed the last of twelve counting sticks into the women's basket. The women lining the field cheered, laughed, gestured and danced in celebration of their victory; the men, rebuked and shamed again in this last match, realized that they had been bested. Amid whooping and playful chatter, all agreed it was time to move on to the feasting and dancing that accompanied these seasonal games of "foot ball."[1]

The game is much different when played at today's Rancocas Valley Regional High School, but the taunting, cheering and bruised muscles remain. Lenape-Delaware tribal members would recognize something quite familiar in modern American football, but might wonder how fair it can be if only men play.

A similar juxtaposition of comfortable familiarities and awkward differences would be evident in many aspects of the interaction of the indigenous peoples and the Europeans, setting the tone from the start. Each came armed with a set of common beliefs and practices that had evolved, over centuries, from dissimilar circumstances. Each, while willing to entertain the ideas of the other, was rooted in customs and beliefs largely contradicting those of the other.

As Jake Page notes in his history of Native Americans, "The question of what to take on from the white man—and what to try to avoid—would become a burning one for almost every group of Indians, and is still asked today. After a period of adjustment, many Europeans found they had changed as well, adopting elements of the Indian way of life in response to the vast opportunities and expanse of the new land."[2]

Now, this is not to say that the game of American football as we know it originated with the Native Americans, or that it had a significant place in the early colonization of New Jersey. It does point to the similarities of rivalry and recreation found within the two cultures. It points to the spirit of competition, and to relationships among work, religion and play, which the native culture embraced and the immigrant culture eventually acquired.

It also points out that most things we believe to be new have, in fact, been around for some time. This is an important concept in looking at the history of Mount Holly and the area—in fact, for any history. Many of the beliefs and concerns we have today are similar, or even identical, to concerns and issues faced by people three hundred years ago.

The effect the indigenous peoples had on the incoming settlers was critical to the survival of the colony. Not unlike the experience of other tribes up and down the Eastern seaboard of the American continent, the effect of the incoming settlers on the indigenous people was devastating.

First Nations and First Settlers

History in North America has tended to focus on the written accounts of immigrants from other continents. Thankfully, through the efforts of archaeology and ethnic studies, we can now read about and learn of our land before European arrival. In the case of Mount Holly and Central New Jersey, this is the story of the Lenape. As with most indigenous tribes in North America, Lenape means simply "the common people," in the same way modern peoples in the United States refer to themselves as Americans.

> *The name bestowed upon New Jersey by the Indians was "Shejachbi" (pronounced as if spelled "Sha-ak-bee"). They claimed the whole area comprising New Jersey. Their great chief, Teedyescung, stated at the tribal conference at Easton, Pa., in 1757, that their lands reached eastward from river to sea. The name Lenni Lenape is not pronounced as spelled, that is, the last word is not. That, phonetically, would be Len-apee, but it is to be pronounced as though spelled "Len-au-pay."*[3]

Rather than a single tribe, the Lenape consisted of several sub-clans and were, in turn, part of a larger group or coalition. All of the related tribes were loosely part of the Delaware Group, situated from the northern sections of what are now New Jersey, Pennsylvania and New York, southward to the Delaware Bay. These tribes shared similar custom and traditions, much as did other tribal coalitions such as the Iroquois and Sioux confederacies.

Many of the Delaware sub-tribes, including the Lenape, were subordinated to the leadership of the larger Delaware and Algonquin confederacy, almost in the manner of medieval fiefdom. Local peace and prosperity was maintained by periodic tithes and services paid to this leadership among the tribes, for which the smaller tribes received support and security. Some might call this the beginning of the "protection" racket in New Jersey.

The name "Delaware" was actually provided by the Europeans, not the natives. The native name for the river, *Lenape Wihittuck*, simply means "River of the Lenape." This really is not so strange if you consider the current name of the river is merely an honor to Lord de la Ware, given in much the same way we now name highways and streets after honored people. The Lenape simply gave the body of water a name reflecting its significance to them—their source of water, transport and food. As indicated by Chief Roy Crazy Horse,

> *Essentially the term Renape refers to us as an ethnic group, a people speaking a common language. However, we were not all united in one Nation. Our people governed themselves freely and harmoniously as independent republics, which sometimes came together in alliances or confederations, such as the Powhatan Confederacy. Thus Powhatan refers to our political identity, while Renape refers to our ethnic/language identity.*[4]

The Lenape settled in two locations near modern Mount Holly. Both sites consisted of stockade villages of several interrelated families and were along the Rancocas (Ankokus) Creek, which flowed from the pine barrens and hilly sections of the watershed into the Delaware near present-day Riverside and Delran. The creek provided transportation, food and water for crops of maize, beans and squash. Smaller encampments were erected and abandoned as needed to take advantage of seasonal food, such as when fishing or clamming near the Atlantic Ocean or harvesting cranberries and strawberries within the pine barrens. Hunting and gathering was augmented by cultivated crops, not replaced by them as in some Southwestern cultures.

> *For 10,000 years the Lenape (Len-AH-pay, "the common people") lived between the Delaware and Hudson Rivers. They spoke a dialect of the Algonquin language. The Remkokes ("many kinsmen") band of this tribe, with several hundred members, lived along a large creek now called by their name. In a fork between two branches of the creek, 10 miles upstream from the Delaware River, was their principal village where their chief, Ramkok, lived. On a 1677 map this village was named Mispenninck.*[5]

Swedish settlers and some Dutch migrating around the cape from New Amsterdam had settled the area before the arrival of the English, and so the Indians were familiar with the white man when immigrants arrived in what would be Burlington. But, since the Dutch and Swedes came in relatively few numbers and primarily for the purpose of operating a fur trade, there had been limited interaction. The new wave of immigration brought hundreds and then thousands of land-hungry and enterprising Europeans seeking their fortunes not in the replenishable beaver and bear, but in the rich and fertile assets of the Lenape.

> *The Lenape lived in a longhouse and huts made of saplings and bark. The families were organized around the female line of descent, with men moving to the woman's longhouse upon marriage. Here they carried on much the same range of activities we do today. They sang and*

Sellers map, 1677. This map, completed by John Sellers, shows the approximate disposition of settlements and Indian villages at the time of the arrival of most of the pioneers of Mount Holly and the area. The village Mispenninck is located below the "W" in "WEST" and is approximately two miles from downtown Mount Holly. The map erroneously indicates that New Jersey is an island. *Courtesy New Jersey State Archives, Trenton.*

E Y
Modus muniendi
The manner of the Indian Fortifications Towns Houses and Dwelling places
Waranawankongs.
Tappaans
Wap:
pings.
PART OF NEW YORK.
Waoranecks.

Typical Lenape longhouse dwelling. Several might be located within a low stockade (see inset detail from the Sellers map), the fencing being as much to keep domesticated animals inside as to keep wild animals and intruders out. *Courtesy Powhatan-Renape Museum, Westampton, New Jersey. Photograph by author.*

enjoyed the music of flutes, rattles, and drums. The children played games and the adults told stories. They had community meetings and religious ceremonies. Nature was sacred for them and they laid their dead to rest in burial grounds and believed in an afterlife that depended on how you lived your life on Earth.

The Lenape wore buckskin and furs, carefully sewn and adorned. They painted and tattooed themselves and wore jewelry. They wove nets and rope from hemp but made no textiles, not having cotton, flax, or wool. They made baskets and pottery and stone tools of many kinds. The Lenape planted gardens of corn, beans, and squash and collected wild nuts and fruits such as strawberries, plums, peaches, cherries, cranberries, and grapes. They ate roots and tubers and had medicinal herbs and tobacco. They took many kinds of fish from the rivers such as rockfish, catfish, shad, sheepshead, sturgeon, and herring. There were also mollusks and crustaceans, and in the spring they went to the Atlantic coast to catch the salmon swimming up the rivers. They ate bird eggs and fledglings and trapped quail and turkeys. In the forest around the village they hunted rabbit, deer, and beaver. There were also large mammals such as bear, elk and mountain lions.[6]

IMMIGRATION AND DEVASTATION

Cross-cultural influence was felt from the very beginning. Mary Murfin (or Murtin), four years old at the time of the landing at Bridlington (Burlington), became well acquainted with the natives, learned their language and lived among them for many years before moving to Philadelphia. Mary Murfin (Smith, after marrying David Smith) spoke of hardships that first winter.

The early settlers arriving around 1677–78 found themselves living in caves and hovels constructed along the banks of the Delaware River. They had arrived in November, without plans for shelter or food. They lived on bartered venison, maize and squash, and learned to fish the river in winter. They used hand mills and stones in hollowed rocks to grind maize and what little wheat they had brought. They followed the custom of the Indians in hunting for food, something many had not been permitted to do in England due to class restrictions and poaching laws.[7]

One principal member of the proprietorship, Mahlon Stacy, was instrumental in establishing Burlington County and the region as far north as the falls of the Delaware (now Trenton). Stacy was apparently well-to-do upon his arrival, having brought several servants along with him to the New World. He quickly became a major landholder, investor and entrepreneur in the new colony.

Stacy had been very influential in the Society of Friends, of which body he was a faithful member while in England, and this gave him a high status among the proprietors and new arrivals. His subsequent breadth of plantation and mercantile interests and his general wealth rank him easily among the few who framed Burlington County between 1676 and 1715. Nevertheless, as noted in Woodward and Hageman, two travelers from Sweden visiting the former Swedish colony wrote of the bare conditions they found at the home of this "leading man of the colony":

> *In 1679–80 Jasper Dankers and Peter Sluyter, Dutch Labadists, speak in their Journal of Mahlon Stacy's house on the site of Trenton. He was the representative man in the vicinity of "Ye ffalles." That establishment was, doubtless, little better than a camp. The houses must have been merely temporary shelters,—shacks, if you please. It was in such that Mahlon Stacy entertained, or, rather, suffered Dankers and Sluyter to stay over night on Friday, November 17, 1679. The Stacys must have filled the habitation itself and Dankers and Sluyter, as they recorded, could find no bed but had to sit up all night.*[8]

We often read of the privations of the Plymouth Pilgrims and the hostile natives faced by the Jamestown settlers. In 1677–78 the settlers in Burlington County were facing the same issues and finding similar solutions. As with most new arrivals, they learned from those who came before, built upon that knowledge and worked out solutions. The interaction with and accommodation of these settlers by the Indians served to sustain the white population, the growth of which saw increased competition for space and resources.

Mary Murfin's diary and journal make note of several other results of this cultural interaction—smallpox, diphtheria, typhoid, cholera and other diseases commonplace in Europe. Europeans had adapted some degree of immunity to these. The Native Americans had not, and died in droves. In that era of bleeding and blistering, purging and sweating, doctors had little or no ammunition with which to battle the diseases. Even herbalists and healers among the Lenape had no treatment.

Mary notes that the natives died in groups and by family, not by individual, indicating a very disastrous encounter with disease. Physicians in London and Paris might have been able to identify eventually the root cause of the calamity, but diaries of ordinary folk simply lament the sickness and show empathy for the natives without offering any real understanding. The settlers were too busy working to survive themselves.[9]

The population of Lenape (and other tribes) in the area was decimated by the encounter with European diseases, with only a few enclaves left by the mid-1700s. Many who survived moved away, first to Ohio and then, after the Chief Pontiac wars, to Oklahoma Territory. Many Delaware and Lenape descendants remain there to this day. In less than seventy-five years—three generations—the once powerful and far-reaching Lenape communities were no more. We had to wait almost two hundred years before the sounds of football rang again through our towns.

As the European population grew and took over the control and management of the colony, the influence of the indigenous tribes faltered. Those few remaining were influenced strongly by the likes of Joseph White, John Brainerd and John Woolman and had adopted Christianity. In an interesting twist, they tended to practice the religion literally, and probably in better agreement with the principles than many of the white population. An example from Lenape-Delaware lore:

> *There was a lawyer in the area who had none too good a reputation for honesty. One of the Lenape employed him to do a little legal business. It was done to the client's satisfaction, the fee duly paid, and a receipt for it duly demanded.*
>
> *"A receipt isn't necessary," the lawyer said.*
>
> *"But I want it," replied the man. There was some argument, and the attorney finally demanded his reason.*
>
> *The man looked closely at the lawyer before speaking, "Since becoming a Christian I have been very careful in all my dealings, that I may be ready for the judgment, and when that day comes I don't want to take time to go to the bad place to get my receipt from you."*
>
> *The receipt was made out and delivered promptly.*[10]

In 1982 the Powhatan Renape Nation negotiated an agreement with the State of New Jersey to take over 350 acres of state owned land in the town of Westampton. The property is now recognized by the state of New Jersey and the general public as the Rankokus Indian Reservation. The nation's administrative center is located here to manage its community, educational, cultural, social and other programs and services.[11]

2.
Evolution of Place

If you look at the surnames of most of the folks who settled Mount Holly it would be easy to see their English and Scotch-Irish origins. Though we have several place names that belie their Dutch and Swedish derivation, it was the English who made the bold move to acquire and sell off the land between the Hudson and Delaware Rivers and send a population to establish colonies. To avoid the intrusion of the Dutch East India Company and the Swedish (and perhaps even the trappers from New France, or Canada) the English acted quickly at an opportune time. The space between New Amsterdam (New York), Penn's Grant (Pennsylvania) and Mary's Land was deeded to John Lord Berkeley and Sir George Carteret by King Charles II, through the Duke of York, in 1669.[12]

> *By the year 1664 there were considerable English colonies settled in the northern and eastern parts of what is now New Jersey, and King Charles II, considering a Dutch and Swedish colony in the heart of his dominions in America to be a menace to his government, determined to dispossess them. There were several such Dutch and Swedish settlements on the Delaware River below what is now Trenton. For the purpose mentioned, King Charles II evidently intended that his brother the Duke of York, afterwards James II, should make the conquest in his name, and on March 20, 1664, by patent granted unto the duke a tract of land in North America, including New Jersey.*[13]

Of course, granting such ownership was a bit presumptuous on the part of the king, though monarchs tend to be that way. A similar arrogance would cause the monarchy loss of these very same colonies almost exactly one hundred years later. For the present, the two astute investors, Berkeley and Carteret, made a simple business decision. They divided the property between them into East and West New Jersey and sent a surveyor to mark the boundary. The designation East and West remained through most of the eighteenth century, and the perfectly straight dividing line, generally called Province Line Road in municipalities it passes through, can still be seen on the map of the state.

Berkeley and Carteret were not disposed to leave their comfortable surroundings in London just to make some additional pocket change. They arranged for a series of proprietor's agents to act on their behalf and manage disposition of their new lands. Some assigned agents completed land sales while remaining in England, some arrived in the new world alongside potential customers and immigrants. Some, as we shall see, managed to garner nice estates from their assignment.

EARLIEST EUROPEANS

Swedish settlers and some errant Dutch migrating around the cape from New Amsterdam had settled in among the Lenape before the arrival of the English, but history tends to favor those with the most audacity and population, and those who win wars. Because of political changes in Europe, the English bested the Dutch in a series of skirmishes and quickly overruled those initial settlers and absorbed them into an English colony. Thus it was a variety of groups from Great Britain and its colonies who acquired and moved into the new land, blended with the Dutch and Indians and beat out a livelihood from the virgin soil, along what became known as the Delaware River.

One of the earliest locales to achieve "place" status was Chigoes Island, occupied by some Dutch planters prior to 1670, along with a few African slaves. Until the arrival of English immigrants there was no place called Burlington, and "Mount" Holly was a bump in the landscape, around which Indian paths wound on their way from the river through the pinelands to the ocean. In short order, a town was established on the Jersey riverbank called first New Beverly, then Bridlington and finally Burlington City, laid out in 1679. By comparison, Philadelphia was laid out in 1682.

According to Henry Shinn and others, one of the first settlers was a Walter Reeves, who established a plantation on the south side of the north branch of the Rancocas.[14] Reeves set up a farm and trading site about one to two miles west of what is now the center of Mount Holly. He then purchased additional land on the north side of the creek and established a farm of several hundred acres there (about where present-day Hainesport is located). Though never pinpointed precisely, the area is an excellent location for planting and for using the creek as a transportation route. The Lenape realized this long before Mr. Reeves, and their encampment at the fork of the north and south branches could very well have been the reason for his selection of this site.

Being one of the first European settlers, Reeves was totally dependent on his own wiles and the good nature of the Indians for his family's survival. We have to assume he interacted with the Dutch and Swedes, but there are no records of this existing in the traditional archives. The family genealogy indicates he may have arrived from the West Indies or from Long Island.[15] In either case, he was one of the few English-speaking settlers already here when the *Kent* and other shiploads of immigrants arrived at Burlington.

The Ankokus was deep, and a good port could be established from which to receive and dispatch oceangoing vessels, allowing trade with other colonies and into the West

Rancocas. View of the wide bend near Long Bridge and Hainesport, which was an important dock and shipping site. *Photograph by author.*

Indies. It is believed Walter Reeves did precisely that, and became well known as a trader and plantation owner, though not someone of quiet and pleasant demeanor. The ensuing settlers tended to find him profane and less than cooperative. But then, such seems to be the case with most first-timers as they watch their way of life eroded by subsequent arrivals.

Local tradition has had it that one of Reeves's daughters [he had two known daughters] married Howell Davis, a Caribbean pirate, who might have visited Reeves's plantation once or twice.[16] In searching further this appears unlikely, since Davis lived only from 1690 to 1719 and spent most of his time off the African Coast; but not totally impossible given Reeves's ongoing trade with Barbados.

Another colorful tradition, again unlikely, is that Davis buried treasure in the vicinity of the Reeves property. The Stokes map actually pinpoints the traditional spot of the treasure. Of course, there were pirates coursing around the New Jersey coastline and up the Delaware River, including the infamous Blackbeard. So, who knows? There may be a treasure buried somewhere along the creek, though the flood of modern construction has probably washed away any indication of where.

We might wonder, looking at the creek today, how oceangoing vessels ever plied these waters. The Rancocas shifts its banks frequently as it passes through the soft,

Rancocas between Pine and Mill in Mount Holly, showing the general width and disposition of the creek at this point. *Photograph by author.*

sandy soil of the area, and there has been silt fill in the creek over three hundred years, so it may have been much deeper than at present. Exploring the size and draft of ships, which sailed the seas at the time, it is not hard to see that they would be quite capable of navigating the creek, even as far as Lumberton and Shreveville. What may be difficult to fathom is how anyone could survive in these ships on the open Atlantic.

The Edge of the Wilderness

Burlington was named the capital of West Jersey in the disposition of *Nova Caesarea* (New Jersey) land grants; Perth Amboy was the capital of East Jersey. Though many of the original English settlers and investors arrived in the Burlington area on the *Kent*, others arrived soon after on the *Shield*, *Willing Mind* and *Martha*. Not all of the travelers stayed in Burlington. Many migrated inland, perhaps drawn by the success of a few early planters like Reeves, as far west as the area of Hainesport and Mount Holly, and as far north as the Falls of the Delaware (modern-day Trenton).[17]

Settlers based their land ownership on the traditions of their home country. Grants of real estate from the English King were passed through favorites in court and allotted by them to friends and colleagues. The Colony of Jersey, bounded primarily by the Delaware and Hudson Rivers, followed this same process in the division of its land

Shin-Curtis Log Cabin, circa 1712, Mount Holly, shows the typical construction of a "house" at the time. *Courtesy Mount Holly Historical Society.*

among early groups of stockholders, proprietor's agents and patrons. Commissioners sent by the creditors of one Edward Byllings of England made a deal for his Royal Grant properties, which section included the location of present-day Mount Holly, intending to sell these to recoup losses in their dealings with Mr. Byllings.

The deed for the lands between Rankokus Creek and Assunpink was dated October 10, 1677, the pay consisted of "guns, match-coats, kettles, hose, petticoates [*sic*], bars of lead, powder, knives, Indian axes, combs, tobacco, rum, looking glasses, fish hooks, jaw harps, needles, pipes, bells, etc." and this was considered a fair equivalent by the Indians whose only title was title by possession.[18]

And then there is the idea of plantations in New Jersey. Often we think of a plantation as being a traditional part of Southern United States locales. In reality the term is applied to any large, self-reliant farm system. The typical plantation or colonial farmhouse now visible in so many places around Mount Holly was not yet a fixture in the early years. Most homes, if they were more than caves or tents, were small, rough cabins constructed of hewn timbers and daubed with mud or clay.

Plantations generally incorporated production of all necessary goods on site and maintained a good number of fowl and livestock in addition to growing traditional crops such as maize (corn), barley and wheat. Additional crops would have been flax and hemp; the one for making oils and linen, the other for roping. Beer would have been produced as a way to ensure the consumption of minerals and vitamins more

INVENTORY OF WALTER REEVE

A true and perfect Inventory of ye Goods and Chattels of Walter Reeves of Rancocas Alias Northampton River in ye County of Burlington in ye Province of New West Jersey yeoman late Deceased. Appraised this thirteenth day of June 1698 by us, Anthony Elton, Chas. Snowden, Joshua Humphreyes, Appraisers.

	£	Sh	d.
His Purse & Apparel	3	0	0
In ye house, seven pewter dishes, one flagon, thre Tankards five porringers, 1 Gill por, one 1 dozen spoons, 2 Chmaber pots	3	10	0
Two brass pans, 2 Brass kettles, one warming pan, 2 skillet, 1 brass stemer, one possett	6	07	00
One Brass pott	2	00	00
One Iron Pott, 2 pairs of Pott Hooks, 1 settle three chairs	1	00	00
One fowling piece	3	00	00
One pair Stillards	0	14	00
Two box smooting irons, 3 heaters	0	16	00
1 Pott rack, 1 Iron Hook, 1 Pitt, 1 Grid Iron, 1 frying pan, 1 beef fork, 2 Iron Doggs, 1 pair of Tongs	0	17	00
Two old axes, 4 old hows, 1 kl spade, 5 horse belts	1	05	00
One Iron Crow, 2 pair of Horse Gears of Iron, 1 Ox Chain and some old Iron	2	05	00
1 Case Carpenter's Tools	0	05	00
Six Trenchers and water piggons, 2 bucketts, one pail	0	14	00
Three pitch forks, 1 pair of Wool shears, Two Collars Two pair of horse gears, 1 bridle, 1 saddle, 1 part saddle	1	00	00
One Whipp saw, 1 framer saw, 1 hand saw	5	00	00
In ye Parlor			
One feather bed, 2 feather pillows, one pair of sheets, 1 bed blanket, curtains and Bedstead, one old cheast	7	00	00
1 chearn, 1 bed box, 1 wood can, 3 sickles, two reaping hooks	0	12	00
In ye Camber			
Two paire and 1/2 sheets, 2 holland pillows, old and new feathers in ye house	8	10	00
One Chest of Drawers, 1 great chest, one old trunk, 1 Close stool with ye pr., 1 banket	5	05	00
Weaver Loom and Gears	6	00	00
Three augers, 2 Iron Wedges and 2 Iron pins, 1 cutting knife, 1 little saw with some smal iron tools	0	12	00
One Cart with Wheels, Hoops and bagges, one plow with iron, one Grindstone	3	00	00
Three Barrels and one Ancor	0	10	00
Eleven Cows and 1 Young Bull, 3 Calves	40	00	00
The Rie growing upon ye ground	6	00	00
Seven Horses mares and colts	17	00	00
Twenty-eight Swine great and small	15	00	00
Three Bibles, The Practice f Piety and two other small books	1	00	00
The House and plantations thereunto belonging	50	00	00
200 Acres of land bought of Peter Daly	24	00	00
160 Acres of land bought o George Hutchinson	14	00	00
The parcell of land in ye forks of William Biddle	10	00	00
	242	19	00

Walter Reeves Estate listing from the Reeves Family History. *Transcription by author.*

Stokes Map, 1872. Drawn from historical surveys and records, this shows the general disposition of owners around 1682. The settlements moved eastward, from Burlington. Note the John Cripps land holdings, "future location of Mount Holly," near the right side. *Courtesy Mount Holly Library Collection.*

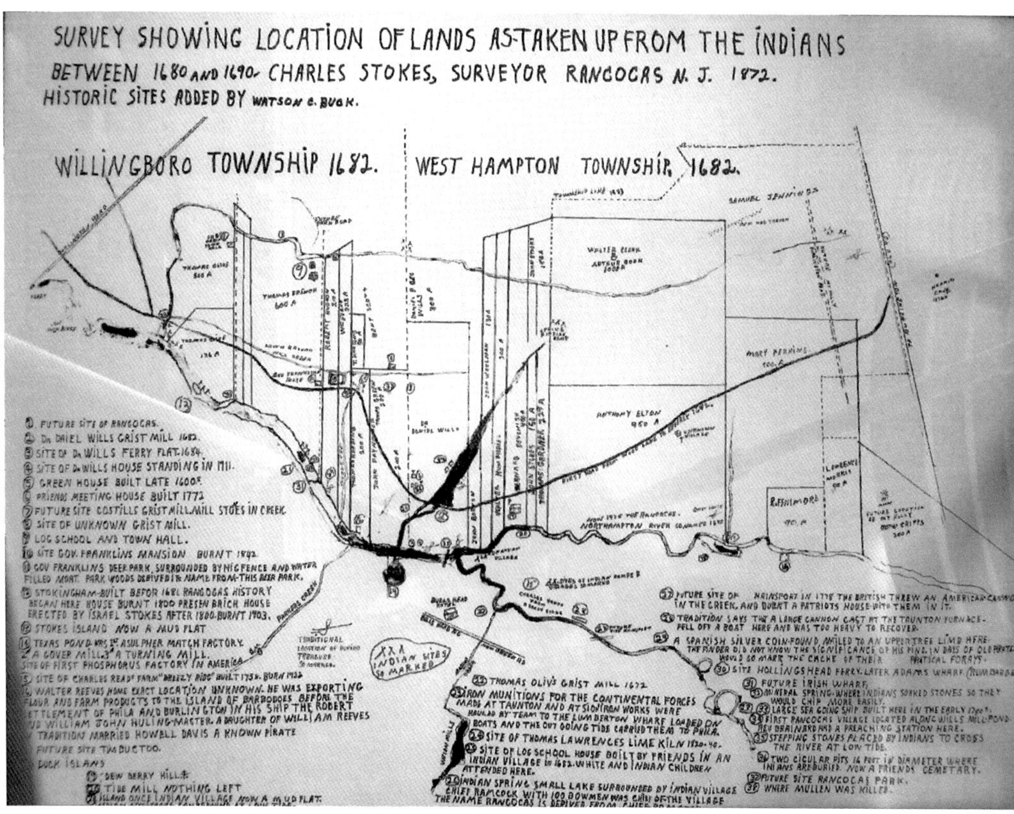

than as a social drink. Beer was consumed by all members of the family as part of each day's meals and was considered essential to the survival of the settlers.

Early construction was simple and functional. A typical layout consisted of one or two rooms with a loft and a roughed-out cellar. In summer months, the family often lived in the "summer kitchen," usually a fireplace for cooking located in the below-ground level of the home or in a section dug into a hillside. Meals were prepared here when cooking could not be done outside, and preserving and canning took place there to "put food by." This practice of constructing a summer kitchen continued for quite some years due to the warm, sticky weather of the mid-Atlantic. Such elements remain a part of the basements in some of the old homes now standing.

The homes and shelters of these first arrivals tended to be simple and plain. Domesticated animals may have occupied the same room as the family in inclement weather. In better homes, farm animals may have occupied a part of the "root" cellar, along with properly secured food supplies (potatoes, apples, gourds and squash). The first homes in Mount Holly were certainly not the fine surviving examples of colonial and federal architecture we see today. Larger homes awaited the arrival of population, greater need and greater wealth. The estate inventory of Walter Reeves gives a picture of the simple, practical, yet effective materials within the typical household through the early years of the eighteenth century.[19]

At this time, the mount rising slightly above the flat coastal plain that was Jersey was the edge of the wilderness—the unexplored region of hunter-gatherers and a few resolute settlers, such as Mr. Reeves. A map by Charles Stokes reconstructing land surveys of the period shows the general situation at that time. Of interest is the subsequent placement of known Lenape villages and camps, clearly showing cohabitation of the area. Also of note is that 1682 marks the founding of Philadelphia.

As noted by Mary Murfin in the last chapter, there was no hospitality club to greet the newcomers and welcome them to their new home with casseroles and flowers and a pamphlet listing the local churches or soccer and baseball teams. Though the Lenape did function as a welcoming committee, in a sense, it is not clear whether they invited the English to join in a friendly game of football.

IT'S A LIVING

In 1680 John Cripps; his son, Nathaniel; passengers on the ship *Kent* alongside the commissioners of Byllings's creditors; and Edward Gaskill, recently of Massachusetts, picked up about 1,700 acres altogether in what is now Mount Holly. Mount Holly was nonexistent as a town, so the designation for travelers might be "Gaskill's farm," "Cripp's Oak," "the Mount," etc.

Since these landholders were the first to improve the land for cultivation, lay out mills, sell parcels for homesteads and develop a plan for governing, they can be considered the first serious European settlers of the specific place that would become Mount Holly. In fact, Cripps is credited with naming the mount for the numerous holly trees dotting its crown.[20]

Cripps Oak. The so-called Cripp's Oak was a prominent starting point for many early surveys, and stood well into the twenty-first century at the juncture of Route 537 and Garden Street. *Courtesy Mount Holly Historical Society.*

Charles Stokes gives an account of Cripps's land in and around the town in an article in the *New Jersey Mirror*, July 13, 1881:

> *John Cripps appears to have been a useful and influential man, and in 1681 located three hundred acres surveyed in terms as follows: "Surveyed then for John Cripps one parcel of land abutting on Rancocas creek southward, and from a certain white oak tree marked with I.C. It stretches itself northeast and by east two hundred and eighty-four rods to a black oak marked I.C. Then northwest two hundred and seventy rods to another black oak marked as aforesaid, from which by a south southwest course it reaches the said creek again through a swamp, wherein grows store of Holly, to a white oak by the creek marked as before, within which tract of land is a mountain, to which the province east, south, west, and north sends a beautiful aspect, named by the owner thereof Mount Holly."*

Cripps and Gaskill took the plots nearest the mount and established the first working farms in what would become the town. Gaskill's Neck, an area where the creek bent back on itself, is a prominent reference point in early maps and remained a prominent location for mills and industry throughout the history of the area, as we will see. For now it is important to realize that developing the operating farm (or plantation) from the virgin forest was a full-time occupation, requiring the work of the entire family and probably a few hired hands as well.

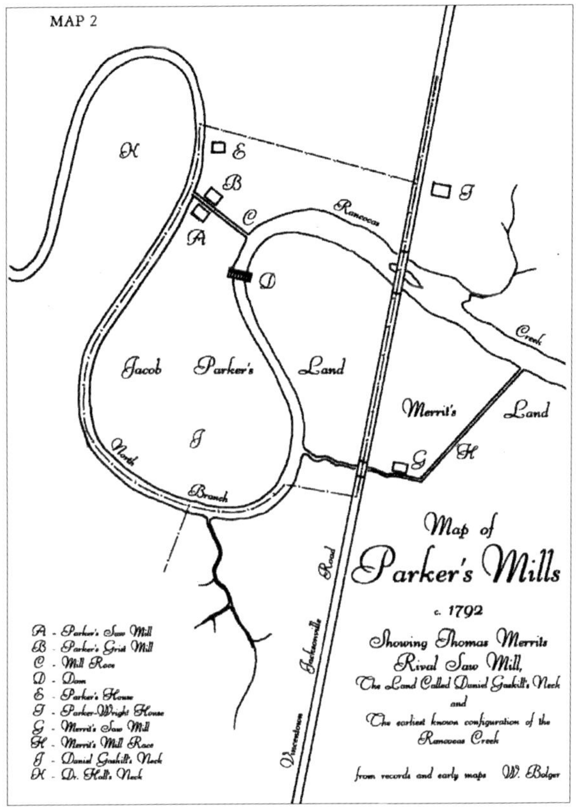

Drawing of the area called "Gaskill's Neck" around 1792, also showing part of Parker's Mills. Of note is the twisting and turning of the Northampton Creek (north branch of the Rancocas), which gave opportunity to dig effective millraces of short distances between sections of the creek. Note that this drawing is not to scale and the distances between points are much greater than it would seem here. *Originally in W.C. Bolger,* Smithville: The Result of Enterprise.

Wood for building was an essential element of any improved land. Early builders relied on an ax and an adz, followed by pit saws, with one man in the pit and another above the log, producing lumber. To raise a town required more than could be produced in this manner, so one principal structure needed was a sawmill. The first were simple combinations of a water-powered wheel, a log shaft and leather drive belts powering an iron saw. By all accounts it was grueling and dangerous work under the best of conditions. Notices in later newspapers of death from accidents at sawmills are fairly numerous.

Based on his inventory, Walter Reeves had erected a sawmill on his plantation prior to 1720 and others became prominent in the area between what is now Hainesport and Burlington. Other mills were already operational in several parts of Jersey, but Edward Gaskill is recognized as constructing the first sawmill in Mount Holly proper. Gaskill spent much of his first year clearing land, constructing the farm and homestead, and securing his family's sustenance for winter. John Cripps and his son also established self-contained farms, acquiring draft animals from earlier farmers in Burlington and trading with the Lenape.

The bends in the creek, somewhat of an annoyance to future generations of lumbermen and shippers, were ideal for building that most essential of all community contrivances: the millrace. Edward (and his laborers) dug one by hand, allowing him to set up a sawmill. It was noted to be at the location on the north branch of the creek between the current milldam and Pine Street. This is most likely not the current millrace flowing through town but a smaller ditch, flowing from a stream on one side (probably Buttonwood Run) to the Rancocas on the other.[21] Edward created a small dam to block the flow and force a current of sufficient power to drive his mill wheel.

Samuel Brian (Bryant) and his son Thomas took possession of the Gaskill sawmill, two saws, mill house and dwelling located there in 1723, but in a land flip that appears typical of the period, immediately gave possession back to Gaskill and three others. These formed a company to build a gristmill on the same site and constructed a larger dam across the Rancocas to harness the water power. By locating an effective dam at this point in the creek Edward created the seed of a town. Another mill, for bolting, was proposed by Samuel Bryant next to the gristmill but never built until several years later.[22]

At about that same time, almost forty years after the arrival of the first settlers, a tavern was constructed "near the mill in Bridgetown." The Three Tuns Tavern, also called the Mill Tavern, still exists and operates as a bar and hotel. It has been a centerpiece of the town since that time.

At that early time virtually everything that needed to be accomplished to sustain life, from shelter to clothing to food, was fabricated by the individual or extended family. Hand grinders produced wheat meal, and wooden hoes tilled the soil. With the growth of trade at Philadelphia and Burlington came more "store-bought" goods, but almost everything from salt to plaster to flour to cider and preserved meat were the result of individual, or small group, labor.

Preserving food was a full-time occupation, as there were no grocery stores from which to get supplies in winter. The first stores, as we know them, did not appear in Mount Holly until well into the eighteenth century. Days were spent working the farm, and there was little, if any, time for social pursuit.

The exception was "first day," when Quakers held meeting to observe the Sabbath. The calendar at the time was based on old English and Roman designations, the first month of the year being March. At each first of the year was held a yearly meeting. In between were monthly meetings, following the tradition established in England prior to the Quakers' removal. These gatherings were the only interaction many people had with each other and were social, religious and business affairs, which might last several days. Meeting took place in people's homes until sufficient membership had been established (through new arrivals or births) to warrant the expense of building a special place for gatherings.

In fact, getting to meeting was not easy. The population was thin and the distance between homes relatively great. For the balance of the seventeenth century and the early part of the eighteenth travel through New Jersey was completed on horseback or with rough-hewn ox carts. Sacks of gain were carried to mill on horseback or with sledges—flat-bottomed boxes with ash rails for runners. The Burlington Path (named by the historians, not the natives) ran from Burlington and the Rancocas through Crosswicks and Freehold to Amboy, the capital of East Jersey. This follows roughly the

Three Tuns Tavern in an early photo. *Inset*: as it appears today. The large doorway is not a garage, but covers the passage to the yard in the rear of the property where animals, carriages and equipment were stored. Though one of several taverns in town, this is the only building remaining with the original appearance. *Courtesy Burlington County Library Collection and Mount Holly Historical Society Collection.*

current eastern course of Route 537, the old Freehold road. The "road" to Burlington was little more than a trodden pathway.[23]

DEVELOPMENT AND SPECULATION

Thomas Budd, owner of large tracts of the proprietorship lands, deeded an additional 100 acres of land to Nathaniel Cripps in 1701, at which time Nathaniel also obtained a confirmation of ownership of 380 acres purchased by his father from William Peachy, another early arrival. Henry Shinn, in his history, does a yeoman's job of relating the interactions and dealings of these first settlers. As one peruses the litany of deeds, sales and transactions of all sorts, reading much like the book of Genesis, it becomes clear that the current spate of feverish development and construction is but a continuation of what began in the eighteenth century.

Land for cultivation was opened on the opposite side of the creek from the Gaskill and Cripp plantations some time prior to 1704, when a Francis Collins availed himself of three hundred acres of land south of the Rancocas. Others followed during the course of the next dozen years, creating that portion of what would be Mount Holly on the southern bank. The new arrivals discovered what the Indians had known for centuries: the land along the creek was excellent for growing almost any kid of crop, from maize and wheat to flax and fruit. The land along the two branches of the creek was rapidly sectioned into plantations, farms and homesteads.

Communication and commerce required the two sides to be accessible, and this resulted in a bridge. The bridge at Pine Street today is the same location (though not the same bridge) as that time. The Long Bridge on the road to Moorestown (now referred to as the Marne Highway) was put into place about the same time allowing better communication between the various farms. However, travel by boat was still the preferred method.

In 1709 there were about 230 people living in all four 'Amptons (Northampton, Eastampton, Westampton and Southampton). Such a sparse population was still largely dependent on the services and supplies from Burlington and other river towns, and the owners of most of the land remained in Burlington or nearby.[24] But by 1773 there were 387 heads of household (landholding white males)[25] and the village was noted to have almost two hundred buildings. One writer speculated that the name Bridgetown was appointed to this spot because, at one point, there were more bridges than houses.[26]

The mount is prominent in this coastal plain geography. Today, as you come off New Jersey Turnpike Exit 5, if you look right you can still clearly see the mount poking above the flat landscape. This was a significant landmark for travelers of the early days as well. Landmarks, combined with commercial resources and civilization, generally lead to villages and the growth of trading centers.

The mount became a gathering place for Northampton-area Quakers, authorized to convene separately from those in Burlington by the Burlington monthly meeting in 1704. The first meetinghouse in the county was at Burlington and so that congregation

First Friends Meeting, Burlington, circa 1683. *Illustration from William E. Schermerhorn's* The History of Burlington, New Jersey.

became the spiritual and temporal leader in the area. Other groups wishing to meet separately needed to obtain the approval of that congregation. The Quakers living in and around Mount Holly wanted to meet somewhere closer to home, and their request was granted.

They first met in the homes of Restore Lippincott, near the mount, and Daniel Wills in Eayrestown. Thinking of the distance between these locations today we might reflect on how they managed to gather on foot and with limited transportation from the surrounding plantations and farms.

In 1716 the first meetinghouse was erected on what is now the juncture of Woodlane Road (then Gaskill's Lane) and Woodpecker Lane (then the principal northwesterly road out of town) near an existing Friends cemetery, which can still be seen. The site had been a burial ground for the Quaker congregation living around the Mount and the mills with it being too far to travel to Burlington City for interment. When the Burlington meeting gave permission for a permanent site in 1716, a spot was selected near the burial ground.[27] Though outside of town, it was convenient to the various members living within a few miles of Mount Holly.

Zachariah Read relates the tale of an old resident that there was a tavern and several houses near where the Meeting was constructed.[28] Surely one of these homes was that of Restore Lippincott and the tavern was that of Abraham Winne.[29] The proximity of a tavern to the meeting, and its likely attractiveness to patrons from among the congregation, may have been an inspiration for Friend John Woolman's later discourses on temperance when he had his tailor shop near the Three Tuns Tavern on Mill Street.

Old Friends' Burial Ground Cemetery, now surrounded by the condominiums and townhouses of the most recent arrivals. *Photograph by author.*

Within a generation, expanding farms produced enough for themselves, their neighbors and export. This raised the need for processing and shipping capabilities not possible within the individual landholdings. Imagine the joy in the hearts of the farm children when someone established a grinding mill near enough to warrant toting the goods for threshing and milling by someone else. This is what took place in several locations within Northampton, including Mount Holly. Logs for the sawmills were floated down the creek from inland. Grain was carted to the mills for grinding, a portion of the product kept by the miller for a fee. Fulling and pressing mills were established to process wool, produce linseed oil for paint and flax seed for feed.

PRODUCTION AND GROWTH

We often view the mill as primarily for grinding wheat into flour. In fact, mill is the term used for any powered source of production, whether served by human muscle, water, steam or electricity. As such, we can find all sorts in and around a town like Mount Holly, including those mentioned by Doctor Read in the upper reaches of the Rancocas, nearer to Burlington. Sometime between 1730 and 1750, the initial millrace dug by Edward Gaskill was supplemented by a larger, more communal

Millrace as it winds through the lower (original) town today. *Photograph by author.*

raceway, which is now evident. This raceway provided water power to several mills of different nature. Joseph White, Thomas Brian (Bryant), Abraham Griffith, James Lippincott, Thomas Atkinson, Ebenezer Large, Thomas Budd, Thomas Shinn and others were instrumental in seeing this take place, and the move opened the town to greater production and wealth.

One photo of an original—though not *the* original—mill in Mount Holly is known to exist. However, through the archaeological reconstruction of other mills and furnaces from the same period we can get an image of what the works in Mount Holly and vicinity may have looked like and the hustle, bustle and noise experienced on a daily basis by the residents.

Joseph White, who purchased the original gristmill of Edward Gaskill and some surrounding property around 1730, was also a well-respected healer and self-styled physician. He was a well-liked person around town, to the extent that White Street was named for him. Being one of the newer arrivals, having come from Gloucester County, White acquired several properties in town and was known for his fair dealing and generous nature. He quickly became a leader in the Mount Holly meeting and was probably an early influence on John Woolman.

Joseph's approach to business ownership and management represents the best of ideas and beliefs that was Mount Holly during the eighteenth century. Ownership

Later photo of mills, warehouses and an old chimney in the vicinity of the original mill site. *Courtesy Cowgill Collection, Mount Holly Historical Society.*

in many cases was stewardship; one controlled the production of goods and services for the betterment of the general community as well as for personal gain. Those who operated business solely for personal gain were considered unacceptable, not successful. Certainly, there were those in the population who managed their affairs solely for profit, to the detriment of their community. But these were people to be feared and avoided, not emulated.

What follows is a brief story from the *New Jersey Mirror*, 1880:

> *Josiah (Joseph) White was a minister in the Society of Friends, recommended as such in the year 1743. On the same day the celebrated John Woolman was also recommended by the Mount Holly Monthly Meeting. Josiah White had the happy faculty of condensing what he desired to express either in his public communications or his private conversation, and his company was much sought after. He and Dr. Benjamin Franklin were on quite intimate terms, as he was also with Governor William Franklin, the son of Dr. Franklin, whose country seat was near Mount Holly. Josiah White imbibed the idea similar to Homer, the father of poets, that there were plants and herbs that grew to cure all diseases the human family is liable to.*

I have been informed that for a number of years of his life he used no other medicine in his family but what he made of herbs, and he was frequently sent for by his neighbors to administer the same to their families. He received the appellation of herb doctor. He certainly was a man of clear and comprehensive judgment, and was well calculated to leave his footprints on the sands of time, and those great qualities were transmitted to his descendants to a remarkable degree to the first, second and third generations, as their lives and their undertakings for the public good (all of which they accomplished) fully demonstrate.

Initially it was customary for a mill owner to also be the miller, with the help of family, indentured servants, slaves or hired hands. He would barter a portion of the product—be it lumber, grain, wool or whatever—in payment for the service. As the economy of the area of West New Jersey grew and cash became available, it became more common to see associations of individual merchants owning the mills, as well as the property around them, and hiring on or leasing the operation to millers. Investors would form associations, which appear to be very similar to a modern-day limited liability corporation (LLC). The usual investors in the industrial and commercial growth of Mount Holly were not the industrial tycoons we imagine from the late nineteenth century, but the plantation and farm owners of the area, physicians, and merchants. Each shareholder could, and often did, sell off shares from their portion of ownership for cash or interest in other ventures in the area. Each shareholder was also, typically, a recognized and active member of the community.

For the most part people were thrifty, economical and reluctant to have to repeat the onerous process of cutting and forming timber and joints. They would much prefer to disassemble and use the pieces of old buildings. This activity is often referred to throughout the history of the town. While one historian or another might describe a location as containing a shed and house and working mill, another might describe several working mills and outbuildings on the same site a few years later. People tended simply to improve, remove, work with or add to what was available on the site selected. The selection of the site was often more critical than the buildings located on them, since most forges, furnaces, mills and other improvements could be acquired relatively easily using local wood and materials. The raw materials and source of power could not.

The following classic (for Mount Holly) entry indicating the sale of the iron works on the south side of the creek near Pine Street describes those aspects believed significant in siting and operating any enterprise (even today).

To Be Sold
Two equal and undivided third parts of a good substantial Furnace, for making Sows and Pigs of Iron, with Utensils fitting to work the same, and a large Forge with good Brick and Stone Chimeneys, well completed for two Finerys and Chaffery, for Manufacturing the Sows and Pigs into Bar Iron, with necessaries for carrying on the same; all Scituate and being about a Quarter of a Mile from a good Grist Mill, Saw Mill and fulling Mill: Which is in the town of Mount Holly, in the county of Burlington, in the Western Division of the Province of New Jersey, and is built on a good Constant Stream of Water 27 miles from Philadelphia,

Typical colonial-period furnace. *Courtesy Friends of Long Pond Iron Works.*

> *and is Water carriage within 3 or 4 Rods of the Furnace and Forge, with plenty of Wood at a small distance for making of Charcoal, and good Coal Houses and Smiths shop...Also a good Iron Mine which make the Toughest and best Bar-Iron about 18 Miles Distance, all Water carriage except one Mile and a Quarter, a Good Road and a great Quantity of cold short Mine, about 4 Miles Distant from the works; a Good Road without Hill in the way, and this is exceedingly good for potting any sort of Cast ware.*[30]

The ironworks in some form had been established by 1715; as noted in a bill of sale Peter Bard of Burlington conveyed to John Borrowdale, brewer of the same town, for five shillings, one-half of four thousand acres with "one-half part of the saw mills, iron works, timber works which said Peter Bard purchased of Richard Eyres and John Goslin."[31] Richard Eyres was the progenitor of the Eayrestown section of what is now Lumberton and one of the major early landholders. We can learn a little about what happened at this furnace by looking at similar works elsewhere in New Jersey and Pennsylvania.

Initial owners of the ironworks in Mount Holly were listed as three partners: Mahlon Stacy, Isaac Pearson and John Burr (of the Peachfield Plantation Burrs). Isaac Pearson was the actual manager and operator of the furnace. Mr. Stacy we have met previously. He appears to have been a very enterprising proprietor, acquiring interests in each piece of land and operation sited and built under the proprietors. It is obvious the property had been well developed by the time the St.

Interior of mill, Batsto, New Jersey. Example of the interior workings of an early mill. Note the drive belts, which are made of leather. *Courtesy Burlington County Library Collection.*

Andrew's parishioners erected their small meetinghouse nearby, on the south side of the creek, in 1742.[32]

Thomas Maybury is the owner next most associated with the ironworks, since it was during his tenure that the works produced sheet iron, salt pans and tools for use by the Continental army under Washington. Removing himself to Taunton Furnace following the occupation of the town in December of 1776, he sold his interests to Colonel John Cox. Cox had a working relationship with the Council of Safety of Philadelphia (the rebel leadership). From the record of the Continental Congress it is clear that he received specific orders from Congress for supplies and was authorized to raise a detachment of militia to protect the works. From this role, and the recollection of the site as the position of rebel forces in 1776, came the destruction of the works in 1778 when Royal Forces passed through town on their way from Philadelphia to New York. The site was "completely demolished," according to all existing accounts, and was never rebuilt.[33]

The site has never been effectively excavated. It was very near the initial St. Andrew's Parish Church and burying ground, or perhaps it should be said the church and burying ground were near the ironworks complex. It is clear, through the work of Charles Read in Batsto, a mere eight miles south, the small works at Mount Holly would not have been very competitive or profitable. There was no value in reviving it when a more efficient works and improved roads made for better production and success in business nearer the source of raw material.

Production was seasonal. Lumber was cut in the winter, when fields were fallow. Wood was turned for posts and rails as the market required. Nails were cut and iron workings completed in between seasonal jobs. Grain was harvested, milled and bagged in the summer and fall. Wool was processed, woven and fulled in spring. As a practicality, and to take advantage of the marketplace, most mills provided more than one service. The machinery inside was changed, or the drive belts moved, to power the various components.

Northampton had a mill located along the Rancocas toward Hainesport as of 1802, owned successively by Woolman, Borton, Lippincott and other familiar ancestors to families in the area. Described in the deed of sale as consisting of a "sawmill, turning mill, clover mill, two story house with seven rooms, a cellar and a well near the door and a nearly new barn on the property,"[34] it is not difficult to imagine the ubiquitous "For Sale" sign hanging out front: "Open house after meeting next Sunday."

3.

Friends and Neighbors

John Woolman opened the shop as usual that day in 1743. John was a well-educated member of the Society of Friends (Quakers). Having received his early schooling at the Friends' school associated with the Rancocas meeting, he grew up, traveled and worked within a few miles of Mount Holly throughout his early years:

> *I lived with my parents, and wrought on the plantation; and having had schooling pretty well for a planter, I used to improve myself in winter evenings, and other leisure times. Being now in the twenty-first year of my age, with my father's consent I engaged with a man, in much business as a shop-keeper and baker, to tend shop and keep books.*
>
> *The man who employed me furnished a shop in Mount Holly, about five miles from my father's house, and six from his own, and there I lived alone and tended his shop.*[35]

John received his business training as most people did at the time, through apprenticeship and practice. It was believed by Amelia M. Gummere that he worked in a retail store of John Ogborn, of Springfield, selling assorted dry goods.[36] John's grandfather was Henry Burr, owner of Peachfield Plantation, his mother's father and a prominent member of the Quaker society. That plantation was among the largest and most productive in the area. John would have been a frequent visitor at Peachfield, only two miles from town, and a beneficiary of education in and familiarity with business and farming from that source. He was familiar with another element of colonial life as well.

> *In a few months after I came here, my master bought several Scotchmen servants, from on board a vessel, and brought them to Mount Holly to sell, one of whom was taken sick and died. In the latter part of his sickness, being delirious, he used to curse and swear most sorrowfully; and the next night after his burial I was left to sleep alone in the chamber where he died. I perceived in me a timorousness; I knew, however, I had not injured the man, but assisted in taking care of him according to my capacity.*[37]

John was accustomed to this situation, though not comfortable with it. To maintain privately his own principles in the midst of slavery was, to him, satisfactory—until that day in 1743.

> *My employer, having a Negro woman, sold her, and desired me to write a bill of sale, the man being waiting who bought her. The thing was sudden; and though I felt uneasy at the thoughts of writing an instrument of slavery for one of my fellow-creatures, yet I remembered that I was hired by the year, that it was my master who directed me to do it, and that it was an elderly man, a member of our Society, who bought her; so through weakness I gave way, and wrote it; but at the executing of it I was so afflicted in my mind, that I said before my master and the Friend that I believed slave-keeping to be a practice inconsistent with the Christian religion. This, in some degree, abated my uneasiness; yet as often as I reflected seriously upon it I thought I should have been clearer if I had desired to be excused from it, as a thing against my conscience; for such it was.*[38]

The presence of slaves in New Jersey was not new. Slavery was encouraged in New Jersey under the proprietor's "Concessions and Agreement" in 1664, which offered sixty acres of land for every enslaved African imported. The following year, the agreement offered forty-five acres for each imported African, and in 1666 it gave thirty acres for every imported enslaved African.[39]

In 1702 the two Jerseys united, and England's Queen Anne encouraged commerce in the African slave trade. Nearly all other states imposed a tax on the importation of men, women and children from Africa to be used as slave labor. Because New Jersey allowed duty-free importation of African people, the colony of New Jersey became the conduit to other states. In 1726 there were 2,581 African people counted as slaves in New Jersey. By 1790 there were 14,185, comprising nearly 8 percent of New Jersey's population.[40]

The end of slavery in New Jersey did not even begin to take place until 1804, with passage of *An Act for the Gradual Abolition of Slavery*,[41] which provided for eventual manumission of the *children* of slaves owned in the state. Trade goods manufactured in New Jersey and other Northern states supplied the need for cloth and shoes for slaves held in the South. There was differing opinion as to whether making a profit from slavery was the same as holding slaves. Active antislavery positions were common and violent dialogue (and the occasional brawl) between advocates and slaveholders were frequent.

CONCORD, CONFLICT AND COMMUNION

European settlers (Swedes and Dutch) had brought Christian ideas along with their plows, horses and search for political freedom. The concept of one God merged very slowly with that of a central or "greatest" spirit, as the interaction of the European and indigenous cultures began sharing space, activities, hardships and knowledge. With the arrival of William Penn's great experiment in 1681 came a policy of tolerance, followed shortly thereafter by a variety of religions, each carving a spot from which to provide counsel and comfort to its congregation.

The relentless struggle to shape a life from the soil and forests and streams meant the early colonists had little time to spend spreading or receiving The Word. This Word was, in fact, as diverse as the population: Dutch reformers, Swedish and German Lutherans, Calvinists and Presbyterians, Anglicans and Catholics all arrived at the ports of Philadelphia or Baltimore. They were met by those who had established the city and made the most recent effort in colonizing and investing in the interior of the area referred to as West Jersey: the Society of Friends (Quakers).

Though the Friends made up the largest proportion of any religion at this time, there were other forces at work in the area. There were traveling ministers from several religions, many based in Burlington, Woodbury or Philadelphia. Most preachers prior to 1740 or so had no regular building of worship, but held meetings in the homes of members. The Quaker term for gathering, "meeting," is the word they use to describe their mode of worship, but it was the term used by many groups throughout this time and after.

John Brainerd, Presbyterian minister to the Indians and a prominent traveling preacher, was born in Connecticut and entered the ministry following his brother, David. He often notes in his diary that he spoke on this or that topic of the Bible to a group assembled at the home of this planter or that tradesman. Brainerd had been heading a mission in Brotherton, what is now Indian Mills, for four years from about 1758, serving a small community of the Lenape tribe that had not moved west. He also traveled far and wide to the many settlements in and around his mission, to the distance of as much as fifty miles. Bridgetown (Mount Holly) was one of his frequent stops when traveling outside of his base.

John Brainerd appears slightly more worldly than John Woolman and he found a need for "discourse and instruction" among many white settlers—English, Dutch and Swedish—as well as the Indians. Perhaps this was due to his Yale University education. He felt the need to explore temporal as well as spiritual issues with his charges, often engaging as mediator for land deals, territorial rights and legal confrontations. He recognized that the welfare of his charges was grounded in economic, as well as spiritual, matters.

John preached regularly in Bridgetown (Mount Holly). This entry from 1761 is typical:

> *Lord's Day, Feb. 1. Spent the Sabbath at Bridgetown; and in the Forenoon preached a Funeral Sermon for His late Majesty King George the Second; His present majesty having been proclaimed, in the Province, the preceding week. Afterwards touched on the happy Accession of King George the Third, and in the close of the latter exercise read His Royal Majesty's Proclamation for the Suppression of Vice and Encouragement of Virtue.*[42]

On February 15, at another meeting, John notes, "I thought it proper to inform my congregation of the late King's death."[43] This illustrates both the delay in movement of news at the time as well as the importance of the meeting (worship service) as more than a religious exercise. It would seem that the disposition of most pioneering folk was not toward any one religion or another but, rather, the sharing of a common source (Christian Bible) and a need to gather with fellow beings from time to time. Meeting time became as much a social affair as a religious one; it was also where marriages were arranged. The meeting was the means by which information and relationships were shared and business conducted. It was the marketplace of community relations in the colonies.

John Brainerd, noting the need for a common gathering place for his congregation in town, arranged the construction of a meetinghouse on New Street (now Brainerd), near the location of the present-day Methodist church and 1759 schoolhouse. In addition, he built a small house near New Street and Buttonwood Street.[44] He regularly notes staying in Bridgetown while preaching there and, from the stories and revelations handed down in oral tradition, it is evident he had a strong moral and political influence on the population. In fact, his later preaching in opposition to the actions of George III netted a retaliation by British troops, who burned his meetinghouse in 1778. It would seem that having your residence or church burned by the British pretty much confirms their opinion of your political position.

DIVERSE MINISTRIES

John Brainerd and John Woolman had immense impact on the society in which they lived. In modern times they would have been celebrities, complete with tabloid gossip and TV interviews. Though contemporaries, there is no indication they interacted regularly. Certainly Woolman would have been aware of Brainerd's mission at Indian Mills (now Shamong), and Brainerd would know of Woolman's status among the Society of Friends and position on slavery. But tolerance of other religions was not often expressed in the form of joint meetings or combined services as might be seen today.

There was no shortage of options for the person seeking a congregation. Per Henry Shinn, Reverend George Shadford delivered the first Methodist sermon in Mount Holly. As was customary in this period of tolerance, he did so for several years using Mr. Brainerd's meetinghouse.[45] Methodism waxed and waned in town for several years and did not take firm hold until the early nineteenth century.

The Anglican church in Bridgetown (Mount Holly) was represented by St. Mary's parish in Burlington and traveling ministers until 1742. The parishioners consisted mostly of the workmen and laborers, while the owners, employers and landholders tended to come from among the Society of Friends. At that time the Reverend Colin Campbell, missionary at Burlington, notes that "at a place eight miles from Burlington the people have built handsome church." The "congregation" at this point consisted of but four families, members of the Church of England. By 1745 it had risen from ten parishioners to one hundred. By 1749 Campbell notes that the congregation had completed the interior of the rough-built church, and by 1762 were applying to the King for their own charter.[46]

Illustration of Saint Andrew's Church near the ironworks, looking over the channel of the Rancocas toward the original part of town. The mount is visible in the distance. *In Elizabeth Marren Perinchief's* A History of St. Andrew's Church (Episcopal), 1742–1992.

A burial ground, a critical element for any God-fearing society, was part of the two acres on the south side of the creek deeded to the congregation. This remains as St. Andrew's Cemetery today, but the original church building was removed shortly after a larger facility was constructed on White Street (now Church Street) within the town proper. Apparently, people had grown tired of walking out of town to the hill for services, and the congregation had outgrown the facility there.[47] White Street, named for well-respected merchant and healer Joseph White, was continued in the naming of an intersecting street (current White Street) for him.

Where people were involved in tight-knit religious communities, as with the Society of Friends, they tended to stay within the bounds of membership. Where people worked hard and lived far from existing civilization, they accepted whichever preacher was courageous enough to venture to their settlement. As religious activity came into second and third generations of the original settlers, intractable dogma of various beliefs begins to take hold and we see the formation of distinct congregations. However, this was a new land with new realities, and the strife and conflict associated with differences of religion in the home countries dissipated here in the face of the communal urgency of survival.

It is important to recall that Mount Holly (Northampton Township at this time) was only a small compact village. The homes and businesses encircled the mills and production facilities near the creek and consisted primarily of that portion of today's Mount Holly situated between Pine Street, Brainerd Street, Bispham Street and the

View from the old ironworks across the Rancocas to the mount, showing the white factory building at the location of the second St. Andrew's church. This is almost the same viewpoint as the previous illustration. *Courtesy Mount Holly Historical Society.*

creek. Of course, there were buildings and homes outside of this but those were working farms. The farms of Isaac Risdon, Samuel Gaskill, and John Woolman, among others, occupied the area around the mount and as far as Gaskill's Neck and Parker's Mills (Shrevesville) and Juliusown (Shreve's Mount). In the other direction, farms ran all the way to the long bridge, with small manufactories located here and there along the creek. There was plenty of open farmland and uncultivated space.

Around 1762 a second Friends meeting site was constructed under the direction of John Woolman and others near Mill Street, and this was used for winter worship. The members finding it inconvenient to travel far out of town to attend meeting, they arranged for this building to be constructed in town.[48] This is interesting in that it shows how, within a generation, the town had gained in prominence and people had become less accustomed to hardship and deprivation. They expected to have some comfort. Where they would have traveled eight miles to Burlington to attend meeting a generation earlier, they could not now travel one mile to the edge of town. The growth and prosperity of the town and surrounding area is evident in the behavior of the population as much as in the litany of homes and monuments.

Home on Mill Street believed to be that in which John Woolman conducted his tailor shop. This building was deeded to his mother and he removed himself to his small farm at Branch and Mill (the hill behind Woolman Lake), which no longer exists. *Courtesy Mount Holly Historical Society Collection.*

ABOLITION

The one thing that should be certain about John Woolman and John Brainerd is that they were scrupulously honest and spoke their minds on the issues of the day. John Woolman's remonstrance to people of the period would hold true today as well.

> *In merchandise it is the custom where I lived to sell chiefly on credit, and poor people often get in debt; when payment is expected, not having wherewith to pay, their creditors often sue for it at law. Having frequently observed occurrences of this kind, I found it good for me to advise poor people to take such goods as were most useful, and not costly.*[49]

He was well respected in the mercantile business in town and in the area, but he had another plan for himself. John Woolman had a desire to be his own man, to allow himself to act on his beliefs without the concern of the employee for the philosophy of the employer or a responsibility to the person paying his wages.

> *My employer, though now a retailer of goods, was by trade a tailor, and kept a servant-man at that business; and I began to think about learning the trade, expecting that if I should settle I might by this trade and a little retailing of goods get a living in a plain way, without the load of great business. I mentioned it to my employer, and we soon agreed on terms, and when I had leisure from the affairs of merchandise I worked with his man.*[50]

John became a tailor by trade and applied this trade in Mount Holly. Because of his schooling and ability, he was also regularly employed to prepare wills and official documents for people in town. This gave him ample opportunity to press his own associates to abolish slaveholding.

> *Some time after this a young man of our Society spoke to me to write a conveyance of a slave to him, he having lately taken a Negro into his house. I told him I was not easy to write it; for, though many of our meeting and in other places kept slaves, I still believed the practice was not right, and desired to be excused from the writing. I spoke to him in goodwill; and he told me that keeping slaves was not altogether agreeable to his mind; but that the slave being a gift made to his wife he had accepted her.*[51]

Slave sales took place at the central market building in Mount Holly. This was a structure with an open passage for Main (High) Street and Mill Street under an enclosed second story that served as a town hall, meeting place and court.[52] Mount Holly was in New Jersey, in the North, but slaves and indentured servants were common goods to be traded and bartered, encouraged by the acts of the Crown. The population was largely of Quaker and Anglican background, with strong grounding in equality and Christian principles, yet men and women were exchanged as merchandise.

John Woolman took the issue of slavery and its abolition to his many social and political friends over the years. His first efforts were with the few members of his

Illustration of Town Hall in Burlington, which shows the likely appearance of the town hall in Mount Holly at the same time based on written descriptions of the building. *In William E. Schermerhorn's* The History of Burlington, New Jersey.

own Society who held slaves. His urging and prodding prompted many to free their bonded and indentured servants as well as their slaves. John became a confident and recurrent voice at the weekly, monthly and annual meetings of the Society, and not just on the issue of slaveholding.

Woolman Memorial Home, built between 1771 and 1783 on the farm of John Woolman above the present Woolman Lake. Maintained by the Woolman Memorial Society of Mount Holly and vicinity as an example of an early farmstead and open for tours. *Photograph by author.*

> *About this time an ancient man of good esteem in the neighborhood came to my house to get his will written. He had young Negroes, and I asked him privately how he purposed to dispose of them. He told me; I then said, "I cannot write thy will without breaking my own peace," and respectfully gave him my reasons for it. He signified that he had a choice that I should have written it, but as I could not, consistently with my conscience, he did not desire it, and so he got it written by some other person. A few years after, there being great alterations in his family, he came again to get me to write his will. His Negroes were yet young, and his son, to whom he intended to give them, was, since he first spoke to me, from a libertine become a sober young man, and he supposed that I would have been free on that account to write it. We had much friendly talk on the subject, and then deferred it. A few days after he came again and directed their freedom, and I then wrote his will.*[53]

John's writings and speeches influenced much of the Quaker system of beliefs and practices. Through his travels into the South to preach and visit, he brought back stories of deprivation and mistreatment, and relentlessly petitioned his fellow Friends to remove the "sin of slavery" from their lives. John soon became the conscience of the Society, and Quakers became a loud voice opposing war and slavery of any kind, anywhere in the United States.

1775 Meeting House. *Courtesy Mount Holly Historical Society.*

Though making up less than 40 percent of the population of Mount Holly, members of the Society made up as much as 75 percent of the county. This common voice, once swayed to the beliefs of John and others, became potent in state and federal politics for years to come, and was the driving force behind the *Act for the Gradual Abolition of Slavery in New Jersey* in 1804, noted previously.

As John Brainerd kept indigenous Americans in his prayers and decried their treatment and circumstance, John Woolman became the conscience of the colony regarding the enslavement of Negroes, and any person. These two, alone, provide sufficient cause for civic pride in the town of Mount Holly.

THE CONGREGATIONS

For the greater part of the eighteenth and early nineteenth centuries, Friends comprised the largest single group in southern Jersey and Philadelphia. Their influence and beliefs reached far from the meetinghouse bench; many members of the group were well-educated and ardent in support of a central federal government with religious tolerance, the abolition of slavery, and support of free enterprise and education.

In Mount Holly, the first and second meetinghouses were replaced in 1775 with the current, much larger facility located at Garden and High Streets in town. The original 1716 meetinghouse was taken down for lumber upon the construction of the

Baptist church on Garden Street, early nineteenth century. *Courtesy Mount Holly Historical Society.*

First Sacred Heart Church on Washington Street, circa 1843. *Photograph by author.*

Mount Moriah AME Church, rebuilt in 1863 after a tornado destroyed the original. *Courtesy Mount Holly Historical Society.*

new meetinghouse in town in 1775 and used by Friend Aaron Smith to construct his hatter's shop and home on Main Street (now High Street).

According to the industrious Mr. Shinn, the first Baptist sermon in Mount Holly came from Reverend Peter Wilson of Hightstown. The congregations in New Mills (Pemberton) and Mount Holly merged when the first Baptist meetinghouse was constructed on New Street sometime around 1800, midway between the little schoolhouse and Buttonwood Street. This continued in service until 1843 when a new church was constructed on Garden Street—currently known as the Presbyterian Annex. About that same time, the first Catholic services were begun in town by the newly arrived Irish living in the vicinity of Sand Hill (Washington Street). Sacred Heart Church is their legacy.

Methodism arrived as well, and other religions emerged during the waning years of the eighteenth century and into the nineteenth. The Methodist church on Brainerd Street dates from the mid-nineteenth century. The AME churches were brought to town by arrivals from Philadelphia in the early nineteenth century. John Brainerd's Presbyterians maintained a presence throughout, with the most recent church built on Garden Street around 1880.

Current Presbyterian church under construction. *Courtesy Mount Holly Historical Society.*

S. Wright
gaines

The first large group of Jewish immigrants from Europe arrived in Mount Holly around 1890, but worship was held at the Orthodox synagogue in Burlington City. It was often difficult to travel to and from services on the Sabbath, so a homegrown solution was found. As discussed in interviews conducted by the late Mary Smith, Temple Har-Zion got its start as a meeting of Jewish residents at the Moose Hall during the Depression, when meetings at family homes became too crowded. During 1940 the group incorporated as the Jewish Social Club and, among other community efforts, provided assistance to Jewish soldiers at Camp Dix. In 1949 the present site at High and Ridgeway was selected, and the building was constructed. A rich tradition of community involvement and leadership continues in the present day.[54]

The Quaker meetings tended to be tolerant of other religious groups as long as those groups stayed in their place and did not influence or corrupt the allegiance of a member. A well-documented case involves Elizabeth Griscom, daughter of Samuel Griscom of Philadelphia, esteemed member of the Philadelphia meeting. Upon deciding to exercise her well-educated mind and defy her father by marrying her true love, an Anglican, she was ousted from the meeting and denounced by her family for refusing to apologize and request forgiveness for her act. So, she continued in her long life as an independent thinker, eventually joining in the beginnings of a spin-off meeting called the "Free Quakers."[55]

Records of the various meetings in southern New Jersey throughout the middle and late eighteenth century are full of discussions and dispositions regarding members who defy the accepted tenets of the group. For the most part this involved those who actively joined in the rebellion against England in violation of the strict rule against violence; sometimes it was more personal, as with Miss Griscom. The issue arose again in meetings during the Mexican War, the Civil War and the two World Wars. It comes to the surface today whenever Friends seek to remove the option of violence and war from the diplomatic process.

The population of West Jersey keeps changing, much as it did in the early years. The new waves of immigrants, settlers and entrepreneurs bring their familiar beliefs and comfortable benefactions with them. Over time, after decades of collaboration and disagreement, of conflict and consolation, these too blend with existing congregations to arrive at something uniquely American—religious freedom through diversity.

4.

The Place Builds a Reputation

We whose names are hereunto subscribed, reposing special confidence in each other's friendship, and for the better preserving of our own and our fellow townsmen's houses, goods, and effects from fire; having each of us at our proper cost provided a quantity of leather buckets, according to the numbers thereof, with each of our names respectively subscribed, each bucket being marked with our names respectively.

—*Charter of the Britannia Fire Company, Mount Holly, July 1752.*[56]

The sociologist Alexis de Touqueville, when touring America in the early 1800s, noted with curiosity that Americans were fond of forming associations. Most tasks, services and problems in a community were addressed not by government bureaucrats and the public treasury, as in Europe, but by associations of local citizens. Subscriptions were the source of funding, wherein each member paid a portion of the cost. Volunteers and part-time workers solved road, water, fire and other neighborhood issues. He found this a singularly American approach to solving social and community needs. There has been much debate over the centuries as to the link between this inclination in the country's early years and the nature and support of social programs in the United States today.

Associations to Fight Fire

Recalling the loosely knit fire fighting societies he saw when growing up in Boston, Benjamin Franklin established the Union Fire Company in Philadelphia in 1732, followed by several other companies in the city. The Britannia Fire Company was most likely influenced by correspondence with those in Philadelphia and from stories in the *Pennsylvania Gazette* (the most prominent journal at the time). Peter Bard (possibly a descendant of the Peter Bard who sold an interest in the ironworks in 1715), the first president of Britannia, arrived in Mount Holly from Burlington in 1751. Being as the dates correspond, and the tendency of associations is to place the founding member(s) in positions of authority, it is likely the fire company was his brainchild.

Original Fire House Relief Fire Company, Mount Holly. This was moved from the location near the milldam to the St. Andrew's cemetery following construction of the new house. This photo was taken shortly before the building was brought back to serve as a museum for the association. *Courtesy Cowgill Collection, Mount Holly Historical Society.*

Besides the leather buckets, the "apparatus" of the company consisted of four ladders and four fire hooks held in common by expense of the company.[57] Several of the older buildings in Mount Holly have a curious hatch built into their roof, usually in proximity to the chimney. Since sparks from fires were the most common cause of house fires, these hatches were installed to allow the bucket brigade to have access to the roof, where smoldering embers could be extinguished. This was, of course, prior to the invention of hook-and-ladder trucks.[58]

Other fire companies followed. Each company was "subscribed" to by its members. As in the modern-day association or company, members paid dues into the treasury of the organization, elected governing officials from among themselves and promulgated rules guiding the purpose and activity of the organization. Modern volunteer fire companies operate in much the same way, though they receive support and assistance from the town and taxpayers not available to the early associations. The current associations in town include Union, Good Intent and American.

The Union Fire Company was organized in 1805. Samuel J. Read was the first president, and each member contributed fifty cents, and the grand sum of $13.50

Union Fire Company on High Street possibly part of a funeral parade (note that most are carrying bouquets) pre-1860. *Courtesy Cowgill Collection, Mount Holly Historical Society.*

was the opening entry in the ledger. In 1896 they moved to the new building on Washington Street, with the old firehouse moved from Garden Street to the rear of the new lot.

Good Intent was organized as the Delaware Hose Company about 1850, with the hand engine located in the arsenal at Grant Street. A freestanding firehouse was built on land donated by William Risdon at Mount Holly Avenue, and the company brought in the first steam-powered engine (pump) in 1878. (In this same year the Washington House Hotel brought in the first rudimentary telephone.) Teamsters from around town would unhitch and vie for the job of pulling the engine carriage, since a premium was paid to the first driver to arrive at the station house to hook up to the pump. In 1887 Good Intent moved to their current building at Garden and Buttonwood.[59]

American Hose was organized in 1858, and among the incorporators was Justus C. Strawbridge, the dry goods clerk who joined with William Clothier following the Civil War. Samuel Read, who is mentioned later in this book, was the first president. The hose carriage cost $225—a princely sum—and at no cost to taxpayers.

Union Fire Company circa 1850 hand pump, picture taken upon its being sold. *Courtesy Mount Holly Historical Society.*

ASSOCIATIONS TO FIGHT IGNORANCE AND WANT

Any Schoolmaster or mistress that shall come well recommended to be of a sober behaviour, and can spell well, and write a good, common hand, may find encouragement for the keeping of a school by applying to William Foster, near Mount Holly in West Jersey.

—Pennsylvania Gazette, *November 2, 1749*

De Touqueville's observation applies to much more than firefighting. Associations were formed for every manner of public affair, including education. Schools were not operated by the town. They were private affairs well into the nineteenth century.

The first freestanding school in Mount Holly is unquestionably the Old School House on Brainerd Street, often erroneously associated with John Brainerd. It is an excellent example of early one-room schools and is the oldest in New Jersey still on its original site. It was not built by John Brainerd but his school was located nearby. In fact, Brainerd Street became the location of several places of learning over the years, including the original high school.

At a meeting of citizens of the Township of Northampton in 1759, it was agreed to raise a subscription (form an association) to establish a building for educating the children. Twenty-five shares were sold and a committee of trustees was selected

Good Intent Fire Company after 1878, showing off their new steam-powered pump. *Courtesy Mount Holly Historical Society.*

(Henry Paxson, John Munroe, Alexander Ross, John Clark and John Hatkinson) to purchase property and arrange construction.

In 1814, after being out of use for some time, it was transferred by deed to the recently formed Mount Holly Female Benevolent Association (notice another association).[60] The teachers included in the Female Association School of Mount Holly report, May 19, 1819, were Martha Hughes, Mary Smith, Esther Rogers and Elizabeth West. This group sponsored classes there until a formal public school system emerged around 1847.

Advertisements for area schools consistently emphasized practical and applied learning. These differed from the earlier advertisements for teachers, with teachers advertising their services to an increasingly curious and literate culture. Of course, schools tended to be either for boys or for girls, since everyone knew that the required skills for each were distinctly different.

> *Education—William Mann of Mount Holly takes this method to inform the public that he is willing to receive pupils to board with him—and the terms of tuition and board will be thirty dollars per quarter, for the youth that are under 14. The Mount Holly Academy will open April 5, 1819.*[61]

1759 Schoolhouse, Brainerd Street, Mount Holly. This building is open for interpretive tours. It is operated by the Colonial Dames of America–NJ Chapter. *Courtesy Mount Holly Historical Society.*

For the most part of the late seventeenth and early eighteenth centuries, schooling was a luxury and not a necessity. Education at this time was still the responsibility of parents, relatives, one's self and of the church. Very few people could afford to send their children to European schools or even the newly developed centers of learning in Philadelphia. Most learning was accomplished in the manner described years later by Dr. James Still.

> *I was about eight or nine years old when I was first sent to school, and this was a new era to me. We went to school only in the bad weather and worked during the fair weather. Our school books were the New Testament and Comly's Spelling Book, in which we learned everything that was useful for man to know. The teacher taught us grammar in those books, and taught us how to pronounce everything improperly, and we knew no better.*[62]

In contemplating American history we often admire the self-taught backwoodsman, like Abe Lincoln, but forget that his was a typical mode of learning for much of the population until relatively recent times. Private schools were the only choice for most people, with general schooling not arriving until the mid-nineteenth century. There was at least one exception—the Quakers.

Unlike some other groups, where practical skills and arduous work dominated a child's developmental years, formal education in arithmetic, reading, languages and writing was considered an essential element of growing up—for girls as well as boys. The present-day Friends schools in this area can be traced to this tradition. The practice also meant that many of the leading legal, political and business minds in the area were members of the Society of Friends.

Presbyterians tended to dominate in the clerical element up to and after the American Revolution, with the large schools, Princeton and Yale, graduating many ministers into that religion. The Church of England, many of whose ministers were educated in England, was another major source of learned and influential individuals. But, in the Mount Holly area at least, the Friends dominated the culture and the politics through most of the eighteenth and early nineteenth centuries.

Education of children took place either at the meetinghouse or in the home of a member. John Woolman, for example, is believed to have conducted classes in the small meetinghouse at the rear of Mill Street, and in his home on Branch Street. These lessons would have been similar to that of Doctor Still, with the principle texts being the Bible and one or more grammar and writing text.

Those going on to further education, but still at the local level, might read history or politics (known as rhetoric at the time) or philosophy and classics such as Homer's *Iliad* and *Odyssey* at the homes of their teachers. Formal schooling in the sense we would know it today would not develop until the 1840s or later. College and university education was primarily for the wealthy, and largely limited to divinity, law and medicine.

Several prominent citizens, reflecting on the success of Dr. Franklin's free lending library in Philadelphia, assembled their best books and documents and placed them into a repository for the general good. The Mount Holly Library, originally known as the Bridgetown Library, was chartered on June 11, 1765, by His Majesty George III of England, through William Franklin, then governor-general of New Jersey. The original charter, with George's "John Hancock" on it, is still in the possession of the library, which is the fifth oldest in the state.[63]

Books were purchased by members of the library association and were circulated only among the members. In keeping with the scholarly and social biases of the original founders, fiction books were deemed improper and immoral and were not allowed. The library (any collection of books and manuscripts) was located on the second floor of the Old Town Hall on Mill Street until 1798, when that building was torn down. The library, along with private collections of artifacts, plant specimens and such, spent several years in private homes. Most of the original set of about one hundred books of scholarly and moral instruction is still part of the present Lyceum Collection, which is now housed in the former Langstaff Mansion.

In 1860 the library was officially renamed the Burlington County Lyceum of History and Natural Sciences. A membership group (association) of twenty-six men each paid five dollars for a share of stock and annual dues of one dollar. The purpose of this society was to pursue the study of state history and to cultivate the natural

Mount Holly Library and Lyceum, 2006, located within the Langstaff Mansion (circa 1830) on High Street. *Photograph by author.*

sciences. The library is now part of the Burlington County Library system and has access to many thousands of volumes of all genres.

Religious and Fraternal Associations

Religious communities were leaders in developing associative organizations and societies. When sponsored by a larger sect or group they would eventually evolve into one of the prominent faiths in the town. Other organizations started for civic purposes, as with the fire companies. Still others were fraternal or social in nature, seeking to provide leadership in the community in one or another field. The many organizations are suitably recounted in Henry Shinn's volume.

For the most part, around this time major religions maintained a primary location (and church) in either Philadelphia or Burlington City. An example is the case with the Methodists, whose primary site was in Burlington City. About 1790 a small Methodist Society was formed in Mount Holly but dwindled in membership until 1800, when only three members remained. About 1805 there was a revival helped by a restored

Burlington City Circuit and a growing membership in New Mills (six miles away) that brought Mount Holly under its wings. The Methodist church in Mount Holly grew into a large, well-developed congregation. In 1832, having met in homes and in borrowed meetinghouses, the congregation erected a new home on Brainerd Street, which was enlarged and remodeled into the present Methodist facility in 1882.

An early fraternal organization was the Masonic Lodge #14, which was established in Mount Holly in 1803–04 and became a fixture by the 1850s. Initial lodge meetings were conducted in the houses of members until the former home of John Brainerd on New Street was rented in 1808, followed by another in 1811 on Water Street and subsequent moves through town. The magnificent brownstone lodge on High Street was erected in 1891. This building was destroyed by fire in 1925. The current lodge is located on Garden Street, across from the Friends Meeting.

Several social and philanthropic groups were formed throughout the history of Mount Holly with the tacit understanding that these were to benefit the poor and less fortunate. One of the first was the Female Benevolent Association. It is mentioned in Shinn's history as being the second management group for the 1759 schoolhouse on Brainerd Street, and reports from the group on progress with the school were printed annually in the *New Jersey Mirror*. It was, for all purposes, an association of women who sought to do good in the community without public notice or personal reward. Founded in 1814 (about the time it took over the school) and incorporated in 1844, in many ways it was the woman's alternative to the Masonic Lodge and other exclusively male secret societies.

MERCHANDISE AND TRADE

The Rancocas (often referred to early on as the Northampton River) served as the waterway to the world. The proximity of Philadelphia meant that most commerce in this part of West New Jersey was focused on merchants and commercial houses in that city. Bridgetown (Mount Holly), because of the surrounding farms and industry, grew into a commercial center and quickly became connected to the Philadelphia market. Initially, trade to Penn's town was conducted through Burlington City, but this quickly shifted directly to Bridgetown as the several landings along the creek were established.

The area immediately around town saw the Hainesport Docks at Long Bridge used for shipping, Parkers Mills for production of goods and materials from the interior (the pinelands) and Bridgetown (Mount Holly) mills and merchants for production and commerce in lumber, linseed oil, iron, grain, woolen cloth, linen and numerous products of value to the city dwellers and those overseas requiring resources from the New World. Shipping to and from Philadelphia became the primary means of transacting business. Since roads were still rough (at best) and prone to delays and interruptions, the creek was the preferred route to market and for passenger service. Barges, scows, rafts and all manner of sail-powered vessels plied the creek regularly in both directions.

It is important to realize that Mount Holly was really Northampton Township and influenced areas now occupied by the three 'Amptons (East, South and West).

The central portion of town, which we see today as Mount Holly, became a hub of activity. It has served in that capacity throughout its existence, but it was part of a larger economic and social sphere that reached as far as Philadelphia and New York. Today commuters who travel to Philadelphia or New York for business are commonplace, but this activity was well known as early as the mid-eighteenth century. It has continued, unabated, into the nineteenth century and today.

William Parker's mills, soon to become Shreveville, were a complex of mills and manufactories about a mile from the center of Mount Holly, focused mainly on lumber production and grain milling at this time. It was developed by subdividing the vast initial lands of Edward Gaskill and took advantage of the turns in the creek at that point to construct at least two raceways for powering mills of several sorts. This location became an important influence on the economics of the area in the nineteenth century.

New Mills, established at the point where the Rancocas headwaters gather from a flood plain among the pinelands, about four miles from town, eventually became Pemberton. The production from these locations was shipped through Mount Holly on its way to the Delaware River, Philadelphia and beyond. The output of mills and factories, as well as merchants, traders, shippers and all manner of community and commercial enterprises, gathered at the point where product and buyer connected—Mount Holly.

Long Bridge, now Hainesport, was a key point from which goods traveled via the Rancocas. Located about two miles from the center of Mount Holly proper, Long Bridge was also the crossing for the road leading out of town to the southwest, and which passed through Moorestown and Haddonfield on its way to Coopers Ferry (Camden). This was called Reynolds Street or simply "the road to Philadelphia." We now call it Washington Street, and it was the principal route through Moorestown to Camden and Philadelphia well into the 1940s.

Wood Lane, coming from town near the present Jacksonville Road and passing the mount on the north, turned northwest and led to Burlington City. It passed many well-to-do plantations on the way, including Peachfield, home of John Burr. It also passed the original meetinghouse and tavern and small complex of homes on the north side of the Mount, which had been pretty well abandoned by the early nineteenth century in favor of the central portion of town located near the creek.

The determination of which pathways would be adopted for road travel was often the ease with which a wagon and load could travel over the terrain. Straight, level paths allowed relatively high-speed travel by coaches and wagons once those became the accepted mode of carriage. Early stage lines of New Jersey were formed for through traffic. Not until around 1750 were internal stage lines established for travel between the towns of the colony. The first of these local stages operated from Coopers Ferry to Sandy Hook Bay, operating more for the convenience of the residents of Mount Holly, Middletown and Shrewsbury than for through travelers from Philadelphia to New York, since the trip took several days. With the conditions of travel at the time—dirt, dust, heat, cold and the regular obligation that passengers disembark to assist with pushing the stage up slippery, muddy hills—every day not on the road was worth the extra shilling.[64]

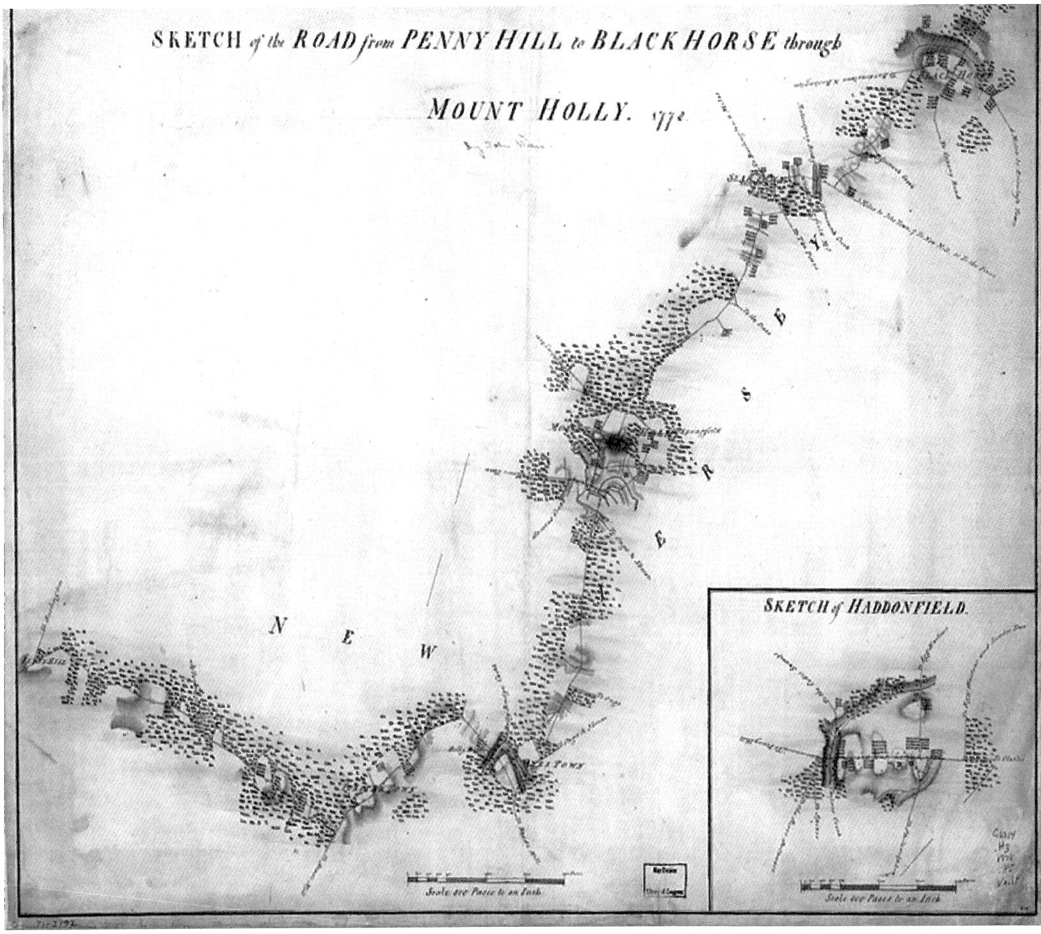

Sketch of the Roads from Pennyhill to Black Horse through Mount Holly by John Hills, prepared for Sir Henry Clinton, June 1778. This portion of the map shows the roads as they appeared through the beginning of the nineteenth century and gives rise to the author's conjecture that the original route from Mount Holly to Slabtown ran along current Woodpecker Lane to Kings Road to Oxmead Road and thence to the current Jacksonville Road. *Courtesy Library of Congress.*

ORDINARY PEOPLE

The workers we often hear little about, other than when some trouble occurred. As these advertisements indicate, we should remember that not all the employees of a facility were voluntary, or even paid workers:

The following is from the *Pennsylvania Gazette*, December 23, 1774:[65]

> *Run away, on the 19th instant, from the subscriber, living in Mansfield township, Burlington county, and Western Division of the province of New-Jersey, a servant man, named Nathaniel Shepperd, this country born, about 25 years of age. Jonathan Malsbary.*

The following is from the *New Jersey Mirror*, December 20, 1820, but might as well reflect activity over the prior century:

> *TEN DOLLARS REWARD—Ran away from David Livezey, a German indented servant man, named John Bender—about 35 years old, 5 feet, 7 or 8 inches high, thick and stout made, light grey eyes, brown hair—took with him a blue cloth surtout, coat, coatee and pantaloons, blue and striped waistcoats, brown woollen stockings, mixed colored cotton coatee, a pair of linsey trowsers, a fur hat, black silk and other handkerchiefs, linen and muslin shirts—several German books, a weaver's shuttle, being a weaver by trade, a bamboo cane, ivory head; two pair of shoes, and a pair of boots with large hobnails in the heels and soals, two watches—he usually wears a white ring in one of his ears—plus other stolen articles.*

We learn that this man is a weaver by trade. That he took with him several German books indicates he could read, at least in his native language. Bender has indented (or sold) his services to this David Livezey most likely in return for passage to America from Germany. Generally, if the indentured person served a specified time, they were to be provided with clothing and a small sum with which to start their own business. Indenturing was also a way for a family to "apprentice" their child for education in a trade, though apprenticing and indenturing are not the same.

As a skilled weaver, Mr. Bender would be in demand within the growing industrial sector of a town like Mount Holly, though he would have to disguise himself and perhaps move away some distance to avoid being remanded to his "master" by the courts. That he left before his contract was completed might indicate ill treatment by his "master," or his intention to start his independent life sooner than he originally planned. We often do not have the details on why someone like John Bender left his employer, but it can be interesting to speculate.

Owning a mill and production facilities was not a sure-fire way to achieve fame and fortune. It was a risk. Many deeds and transfer agreements recorded in the newspapers or clerk's office indicate one partner or another liquidating his portion of ownership for cash to settle extended debts. One example stands out and exemplifies the competitive nature of farming and production in the area for this early period. The stories of Jacob Parker's forlorn existence in town have been part of the legend of the place, but legends often do not address the full scope of personal and family tragedies that they embrace.

Jacob Parker was a successful farmer, sawyer and miller and the owner of a large lot of waterfront and tillable property at the point of Gaskill's Neck on the Rancocas. He became embroiled in almost ten years of poorly planned lawsuits with his neighbors over water rights, millrace easements and dams. His business faltered and he was forced to move into Mount Holly, living destitute in a small shack on Brainerd Street with his son. His wife, Sarah, left him (perhaps this occurred prior to his business's demise) and lived separately in a house on Mill Street.

The descent of Parker's holdings began with the construction of a small millrace by neighbor Thomas Merritt which needed to vent wastewater after supplying power to the mill wheels.[66] This was occasioned by Parker's refusal to allow Merritt to construct a second dam on a portion of the creek Parker deemed his own. The pond created by Parker's dam flooded a portion of Merritt's property. Merritt decided to run his waste-way across Parker's property and constructed this millrace so that it was making use of the water collected by Parker's dam on the Rancocas. Parker, irritated that Merritt was using water supplied by his own dam and running wastewater through his property without permission, opened the dam and dried up the supply of water for Merritt's mill. The mill was now useless.

There ensued a series of actions and counter-actions, the likes of which would make for a very comedic film, if it had not been that each party was now bound and determined to see the other fail. Parker sued Merritt, who constructed a dam above Parker's to cut the supply and redirect it. Parker released his water by opening the floodgates, to which Merritt responded by sending laborers above the dam to float hay and straw down stream to clog the gate machinery. In the meantime, area loggers were taking sides because the dispute was interrupting their transport of logs to the sawmills in Mount Holly.

Parker tried to partner with one John Mullen to revitalize his land and production but was shorted of rent and payment by his partner. Mullen simply entered into the fray of lawsuits draining Parker of his assets. In the long run, Jacob exhausted his funds and energy on these lawsuits. He lost because Merritt was more resourceful in developing political allegiances and better able to sustain legal costs, and because Parker opened a second front in his failed efforts with John Mullen. He retired to a small shack at Brainerd Street and Buttonwood with his son, Jacob Jr., who had mental disabilities. His wife, Sarah, lived on Mill, a few doors away.

By the time of the American Revolution, Mount Holly was a recognized center for trade and commerce in the Central Jersey region. It was the gateway to the resources of the southern shore region and the pinelands. Improved roadways connected it to Philadelphia (through Moorestown to Coopers Ferry) and to Burlington (to Reeves Ferry and the Pennsylvania post road to Philadelphia at Bristol). Regular stagecoach (mail coach) service was in place.

The principal focus of interaction was with Philadelphia, hence the significance of the news from that place arriving by the coach. There was early communication by means of boat travel along the Rancocas and Philadelphia newspapers brought by travelers from Burlington and other places.

This link is important to understand because of the influence it has had over time on the families and individuals living in Mount Holly. When trade began to focus on the growing city of Philadelphia, shipping along the Rancocas became mostly used to transporting goods and people to Philadelphia, where larger ships would take over for the trip to the Caribbean or Europe. Mills and manufactories, such as those found in Mount Holly, took on the role of producing materials for export as well as for local use and a merchant class evolved. Economic prominence, the importance of the Mount Holly meeting in the regional Quaker community, combined with a convergence of roads and bridges, would give the town a recurring role in the growing disagreement between England and its American colonies.

5.

The Battle of Mount Holly

Rebellion and Aftermath

This great misfortune, which surely caused the utter loss of the Thirteen splendid provinces of the Crown of England, was due partly…to the fault of Colonel Donop, who was led by the nose to Mount Holly by Colonel Griffin and detained there by love…Thus the fate of entire kingdoms often depends upon a few blockheads and irresolute men.

—Jaeger Captain Johann Ewald recording the events of the Hessian defeat at Trenton in December, 1776.[67]

Rebellion came to Mount Holly in much the same way it did to the rest of the Mid-Atlantic. Unlike Boston, which had been occupied for up to two years (following the infamous Tea Party and riots), Mount Holly and its surrounding area had been free of troops. Local militia was under the control of Royal Governor William Franklin, who happened to be Ben's son. Shortly after the First Continental Congress met William, he was tossed out by the Committee of Safety of New Jersey. His home in Burlington [Green Bank] was purchased by Margaret Morris, a widow and well-connected member of the Society of Friends.

Despite this political upheaval, trade and merchandising continued much as it had before, but the flames of civil war were brewing. It is important to remember that this was a civil war, being no more exemplified than that William Franklin, royal governor, refused to side with his father, a member of the Continental Congress and an avid Patriot.

Loyalists (labeled Tories by the Patriots) and Patriots (labeled Rebels by the Loyalists) were in every hamlet and town. The schoolchild's premise that all of America wanted to be free of the yoke of British rule is simply not true. There was severe disagreement as to the extent and degree of separation. There were fist fights and boycotts initially, and eventually an ongoing campaign of destruction and assault from each side on the other. Several families in Mount Holly had members who left to fight with Washington's army or with one or more of the Loyalist battalions being formed in New York.

Local militia came under the control of a "Committee of Safety," functioning much in the manner of a revolutionary council replacing royal authority at the local and regional levels in places where the majority of the population was opposed to the king. Until the state of New Jersey arose from the ashes of the early revolution, the Committee of Safety was the authority in all matters civil, military and economic within the town. Local Patriot militia were engaged in rooting out Loyalists from their communities and commandeering their goods and land in the name of the Congress.

Alternative groups were formed as Loyalist battalions where the majority of a population preferred to remain in allegiance to the king. These militia companies roamed far and wide, sometimes blending with others to form larger battalions, and wreaked havoc on Patriots throughout the area. These militia moved into areas controlled by Patriot militia when those were on call elsewhere and took property and goods in the name of the king.

Of course, the chaos and disorder brought about by the war opened up opportunity for another group—bandits. Both sides write of annoying, and occasionally deadly, encounters with highwaymen, thieves, robbers, cheats and assorted scalawags. As with any situation where civil order is disrupted, less scrupulous members of society emerge.

There was even the possibility that one would be recruited into the British Army. Recruiting officers would move into larger towns with the troops and secure "volunteers" through the ruse of offering drink and a guinea and a half (a silver coin) to the unwary, who were then shanghaied into the regiment as a result of "taking the King's Shilling." Their premise was the following decree:

> *On 16 December, 1775, the War Office gave notice in the* London Gazette, *the official organ of the army, that "during the Continuance of the Rebellion now subsisting in North America, every Person, who should enlist as a soldier in any of His Majesty's Marching Regiments of Foot, should be entitled to his Discharge at the end of Three Years, or at the end of said Rebellion, at the option of His Majesty."*[68]

Although no mention of the fact was made in the proclamation, a bounty of one guinea and a half was the required payment to every volunteer.

In between, for the most part, were the Quakers, who had a vow of nonviolence. There were exceptions, wherein members were "read out" of the meeting for joining the militia or other wartime activity on either side. David Claypoole, son of William Claypoole of Mount Holly, and brother of the third husband of Betsy Ross, John Claypoole, wrote in 1826:

> *An elder Brother* [John] *and myself, then 19 years old, Converted our fowling Pieces into Muskets, by the addition of bayonets and iron ram-rods; and providing ourselves with the necessary accoutrements, &c, at our own expense,—were amongst the first to enroll ourselves as Privates in Captain Mifflin's Company of Infantry in the city of Philadelphia.*[69]

Early records show that William and Elizabeth Claypoole were members of the Mount Holly Meeting, indicating that their sons were raised in the Society of Friends.[70] There

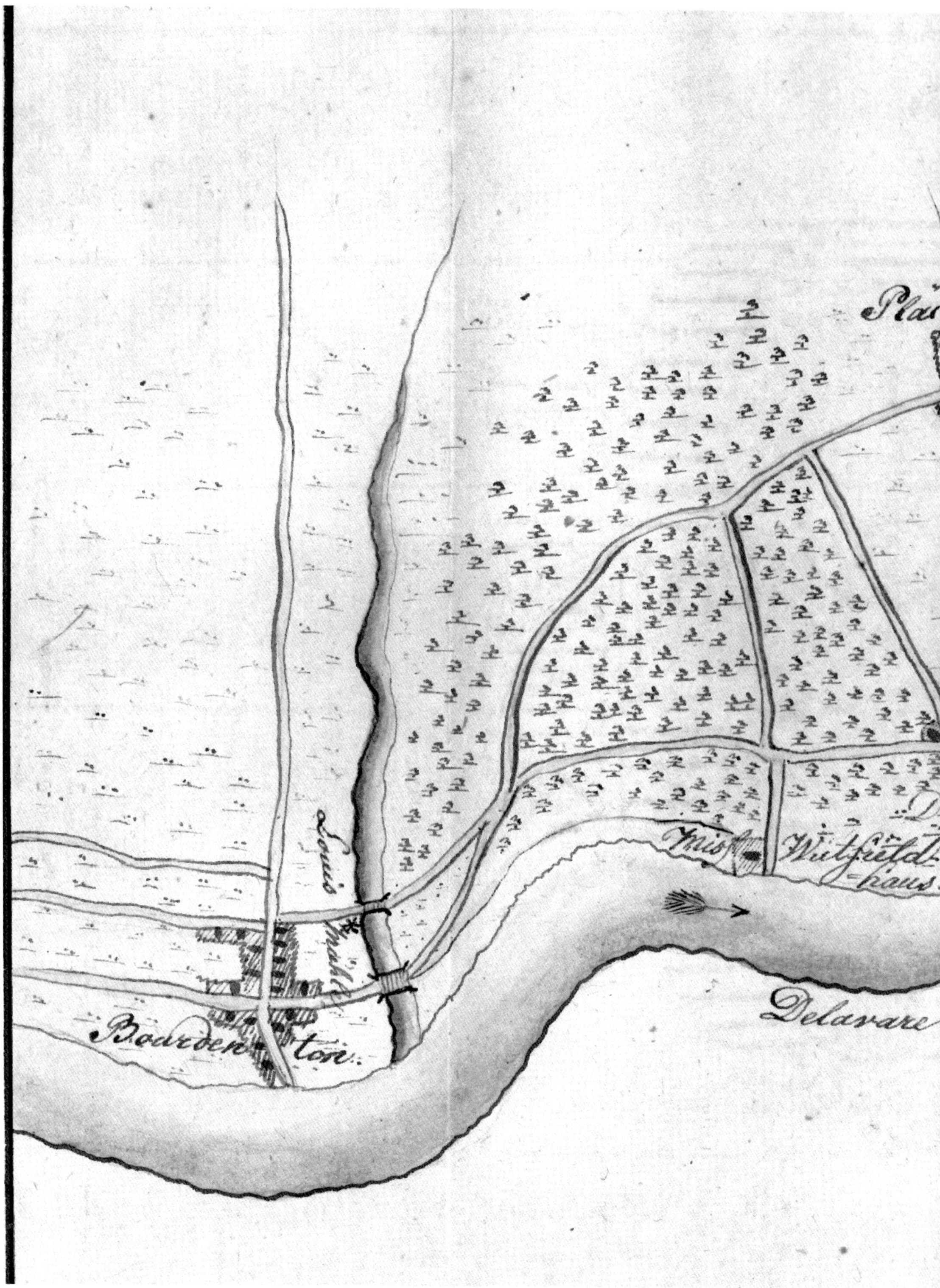

Captain Johann Ewald map of Bordentown to Burlington and Mount Holly, 1776, showing the area where this action took place. Illustration from Ewald's Diary. *Courtesy Joseph Tustin Collection, Harvey A. Andruss Library, Bloomsburg University, by permission.*

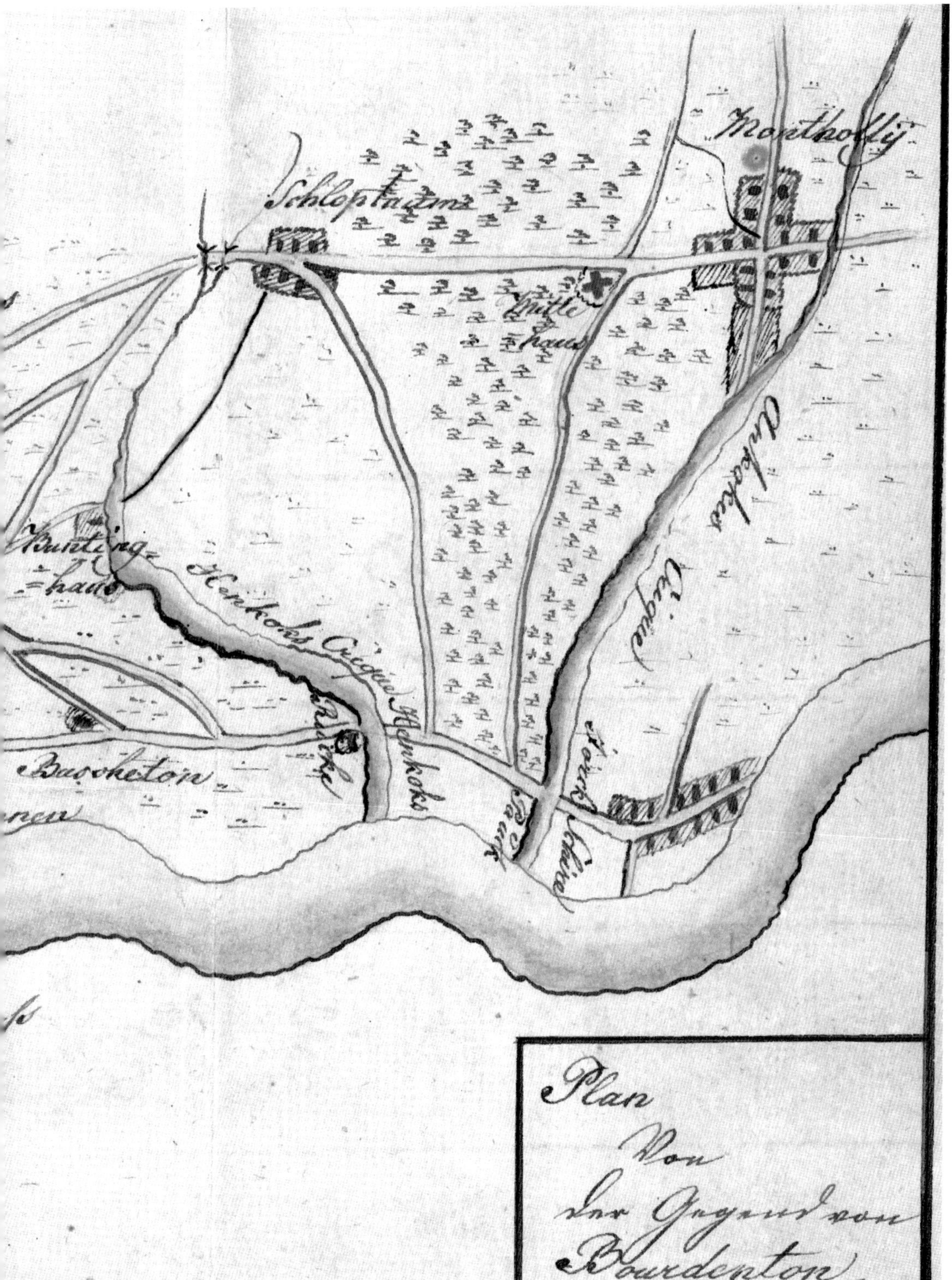
Plan
Von
der Gegend von
Bourdenton

Example of American Militia during annual reenactment of the battle. There was often little to distinguish bands of militia of either side until later in the war. *Photograph by author.*

may be a record in the monthly meeting minutes expelling brothers David and John, in the manner of Elizabeth Griscom, but none has been located so far. Suffice it to say that these were "times that try men's souls," as Thomas Paine was about to publicize.

Many people in New Jersey and the countryside outside of Philadelphia simply wanted to go their own way. They wanted to continue farming and raising families regardless of who was in charge. The merchants of Mount Holly, now a blossoming economic site, were concerned that the war would inflate currency or eliminate opportunity for shipping goods and importing merchandise. The area around Mount Holly was less than adamantly in favor of separation from the Crown until December of 1776.

THE RETREAT

In December of 1776, the fledgling American Revolution was barely sustained by a rickety and rundown army of about five thousand disheveled and unsupported soldiers. Congress had declared independence in July, six months earlier. The army responded to that call to arms by immediately collapsing and losing every battle on its long retreat from Long Island through Jersey to the Pennsylvania shore of the Delaware River. Royal forces pushed the colonial troops south through New Brunswick, Princeton and Trenton, and proceeded to require oaths of allegiance from all persons in their path. This sent a panic into the delegates, the Patriotic public and the economy.

Mount Holly would not have been immune to this panic. Margaret Morris's diary[71] clearly points to incidents in the town where merchants are seen selling out and moving away, and families are leaving with all of their possessions. People sold their livestock to neighbors and left. The roads (such as they were) would have been clogged in one direction or the other leading from town.

The British, satisfied that they had taken the steam out of the rebellion, set up a series of outposts and settled in for the winter. The Howe brothers planned to wait for spring to roust Washington and make a final push to Philadelphia to end the war. There was notable grumbling among the lesser generals because General Lord Cornwallis had gone to New York to join General Howe in the winter season of parties and concerts at that place, leaving them to wallow in the countryside without sufficient Madeira or suitable entertainment.

Adding to the leadership's general misery, they found the small colonial towns were incapable of providing sufficient housing for the masses of troops. This situation was particularly noted in the messages sent by Colonel von Donop of the Hessian corps to his superiors.[72] That meant the commanders had to become creative in their assignments in order to house and provision their troops; they had to stretch their orders. This independent action would result in much chagrin for General Howe—as we shall see.

THE BATTLE OF MOUNT HOLLY

On a cold, blustery day in December 1776, just before Christmas, a small band of Patriots commanded by Colonel Samuel Griffin crossed the Delaware near present-day Camden. Once across, Colonel Griffin secured the services of several captains of militia from Gloucester and Salem Counties for the next few weeks. He also had the use of four small three-pound cannons manned by Virginia colony regulars.

Griffin was fully aware of the situation, having been briefed by General Israel Putnam, commanding the Philadelphia defenses. The colonial army under General George Washington huddled in makeshift camps on the western edge of the Delaware River. The cause, as it is referred to, is all but lost. General Washington, according to Putnam and Joseph Reed, adjutant to Washington, knew he could survive the loss of New York, New Brunswick and even the capital at Philadelphia. But he must not venture the loss of the army. That would spell the end to the brief rebellion, and the experimental government, after only six months in existence.[73]

At the same time, a prolific writer of political broadsides, Thomas Paine, completed and printed his pamphlet called *The Crisis*. Paine wrote, "The summer soldier and the sunshine patriot will, in this crisis, shrink from the service of their country; but he that stands by it now, deserves the love and thanks of man and woman." His words are written in a style typical of the period—testing those who retreat in the time of need. Many people read this treatise and didn't want to be considered cowards, or disloyal. Washington had the entire work read to all members of the army throughout the colonies. The result was significant.[74]

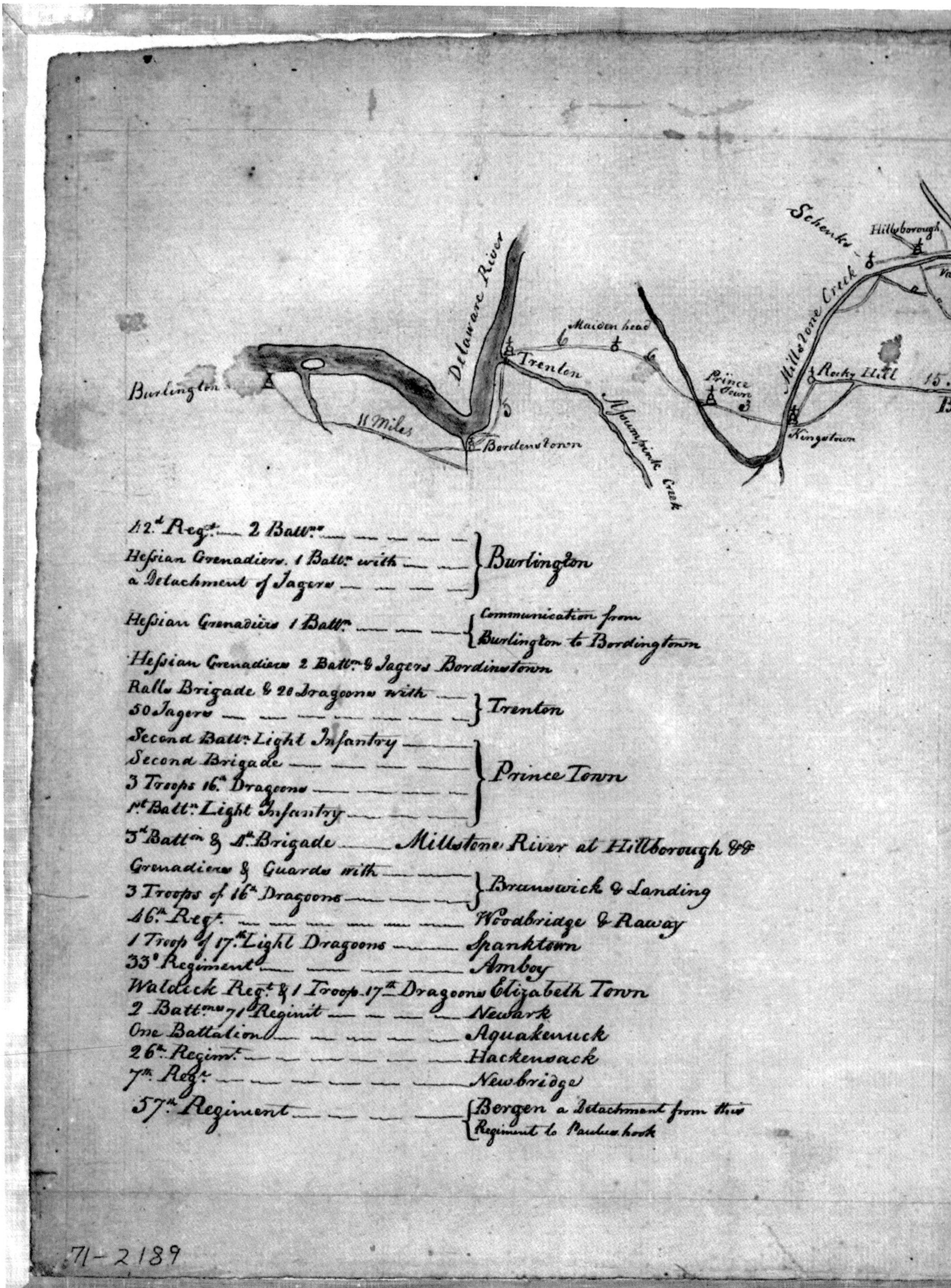

Howe map of outposts. Note the location of Hessian and Scots troops in Burlington, eight miles from Mount Holly. These were placed in position to support the troops in Trenton. *Courtesy Library of Congress.*

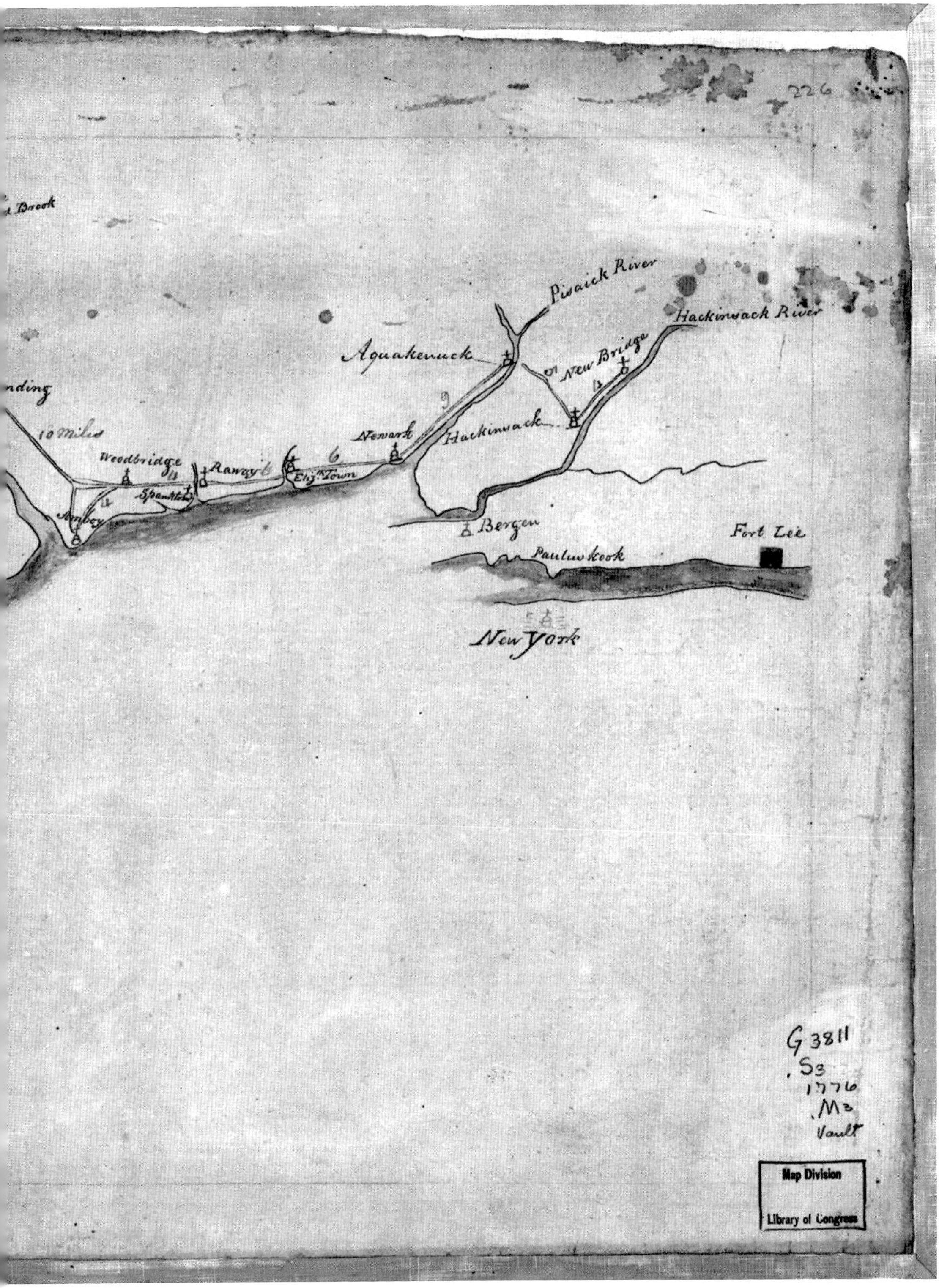
Pisaick River
Hackinsack River
Aquakenuck
New Bridge
Newark
Hackinsack
10 Miles
Woodbridge
Raway
Eliz.th Town
Amboy
Bergen
Fort Lee
Paulus Hook
New York
Map Division
Library of Congress

Recruitment for the colonial regiments, which had trickled to almost nothing, rose again. Battalions in the field started to receive replacements and soldiers who had talked of resigning stayed on instead. Eager to show their patriotism, bands of militia men began rooting everywhere in southern Jersey for Loyalists and enemies of the cause. No one wanted to look like he was letting his neighbors down. The mood was right for the fortunes of war to change.

With this new support, Washington arrives at a daring and risky plan. He knows this public backing will die down as quickly as it arose. A quick, decisive victory would stiffen the resolve of the Patriot cause. He decided to make a bold move to defeat part of the Royal forces who were out of position and unsupported. The garrison at Trenton, across the Delaware River from his position, offered a tempting target.

The British, Hessian and Scottish troops (several regiments, including mounted infantry called dragoons) were placed by General Howe in a position to support each other. The two main Hessian camps were commanded by Colonel Johannes Rall (Trenton) and Count Karl Emil Kurt Von Donop (Bordentown). Count Von Donop also has a full regiment of Scottish Highland troops with him, the now-famous Black Watch under Colonel Stirling, a company of Hessian Field Jaegers (rangers) and several six-pound cannons. He maintained patrols and temporary garrisons at Burlington City, Black Horse (Columbus) and Bustleton (Florence). He used the Jaeger company as scouts. The whole arrangement allows each group to reinforce the others if they are attacked—for the moment.

Washington had ordered two smaller groups over the river at Burlington to decoy Von Donop away from Trenton. These two battalions, under Generals Cadwalader and Read, failed to cross because of ice flows and rapid currents. The gunboats of the Pennsylvania navy (a flotilla of barges with mortars on board) had harassed the Scots to the point where they left Burlington and moved in with Von Donop in Bordentown, increasing his concern about provisioning the troops.

Washington, unaware that support was still in place for Trenton, prepared his soldiers to launch the attack. Without bait to decoy them away, the two thousand Hessian and Scottish troops in Bordentown were a quick two-hour march from Trenton. If the attack on Trenton failed, and letters from Washington are clear on this, the general was ready to resign and leave the field in disgrace.[75] What could change the course of events in time to save the young republic?

Remember Colonel Griffin? Colonel Griffin and his nine hundred or so militia, artillerymen and camp followers (called "distaff") wound their way from Moorestown to Mount Holly on December 20. Mount Holly controlled the most crossings of the Rancocas at this time, and had good ground from which to initiate an engagement. Griffin immediately set up a fortified position among the ironworks on the south side of the Rancocas creek and on a hill now known locally as Top-e-Toy. Sensing something was afoot, the townspeople began gathering their belongings and moving out of town to homes of friends and relatives.

On December 22, Griffin sent a group of about six hundred men (more than half his force) to attack a sentry post at Petticoate Bridge south of Black Horse. The Scots

Battle in the streets with nowhere to go. *Courtesy R.F. D'Entrement.*

Budd House on White Street. One scene of fighting and looting that day. *Courtesy R.F. D'Entrement.*

at the post were surprised and driven back, but they were saved by the timely arrival of the Jaegers and some dragoons. Word got back to Colonel Von Donop, who was understandably upset at the gall of these upstart farmers. He decided to punish them and teach them a lesson. In a fit of rage, against his orders, he took all of his troops and marched them to Mount Holly.

On the way they easily defeated the militia, pushing the Americans all the way through Mount Holly and across the creek to their fortified hilltop (now called Iron Works Hill). The Hessian cannons set up on the Mount at one end of town and bombarded the colonials on the other side of the creek, who shot back with their smaller cannons. On the next day, Christmas Eve, 1776, Von Donop sent the Jaegers to push the colonials out of their trenches, but the Americans were gone. They had slipped away in the night and made their way back to Moorestown.

The Royal forces celebrated by looting Mount Holly and drinking whatever beer, wine or cider could be found. Story has it that they destroyed the brewery next to Mr. Budd's house on White Street and ransacked Aaron Smith's home on High Street. In the meantime, Colonel Von Donop decided he liked the town, particularly a young widow he had found living in the home he had chosen as his headquarters. He decided to stay on for a few days. His officers argued that Colonel Rall, in Trenton, was left exposed. They pressed for some of the troops to be sent north to Bordentown. All were ignored by an egotistical commander more concerned with celebrating the holiday with a pretty companion than with sticking to his duty.[76]

On December 26, 1776, Von Donop received a worn, tired courier on a lathered horse. "Rall is attacked. The Americans have captured all of our troops," said the courier. Reading the dispatch, Von Donop had no doubt. Washington's attack at Trenton was a complete success. The boar had turned on the hunters. And there was nothing he could do about it; he was too far away.

Had he gone back to Bordentown the previous day, he would have been only two hours march from helping Colonel Rall repel the attack, and the result at Trenton quite probably would have been a defeat for Washington, spelling the end of his military career and possibly the entire movement. Here, in Mount Holly, von Donop was eight hours' march away, and of no help at all. Griffin's task was a success, but only because of the wiles of a certain unknown widow, who kept the Hessian commander entertained and delayed an extra day and a half.

Washington's attack at Trenton, and his victory at Princeton a week later, turned the tide of the revolution in favor of the colonials. The rest, as they say, is history.

The Royal forces passed through town once again in June of 1778, this time under the command of Sir Henry Clinton. In typical fashion they made extensive rough use of the buildings and stables, assigned the regimental butchers to the meetinghouse to carve up the beeves for the day's rations and burned John Brainerd's church out of anger over his speeches and writings in favor of independence. They also marched, over the bridge they could not force eighteen months earlier, to the site of the old militia encampment and burned the ironworks. This part, at least, was fair game, as it had been supplying the American army with iron pots and implements. On their way out of town they mocked the few

Original Burlington County Court House, constructed in 1796. This building remains in use as a courthouse and occasional tours are arranged through the County Office of the Courts. *Photograph by author.*

Washington House (Polhemus's Tavern), circa 1860. Much of the appearance of the original building remains in this early photograph. Notice the early electric street lamp. *Courtesy Mount Holly Library.*

residents remaining and promised to wreak further havoc on those who refused to return to the fold of the Crown.

Mount Holly appears to have had a deleterious effect on Royal forces during the Revolution. Perhaps there's something in the water here. Following their less-than-friendly visit to town in June of 1778, Clinton's haughty troops marched off to Freehold, where they were soundly taken to task by the American army at the Battle of Monmouth.

AFTERMATH

Mount Holly returned to its commercial and agricultural roots following the Revolution, as part of the new State of New Jersey. By 1820 it had become the hub of commerce and trade in the Burlington County area. It was the gateway to the pineland region and its multitude of furnaces and farms. It was a principal stop on the stage lines from Philadelphia and Burlington through to the Jersey Shore, a newly opened mecca for recreation and water sports. It was a terminus for shipping along the Rancocas Creek, with barges and even the occasional steamboat making regular trips. And it had one more claim to fame that had occurred in 1796—it was the new county seat.

Being named the county seat made Mount Holly the center of Burlington County activity and action throughout the nineteenth and twentieth centuries. Burlington lost out (for which its residents never forgave Mount Holly) because a location closer to the shore regions of the county was needed. The courts and lawyers competed with the existing merchants and residents in occupying all available space. A building boom occurred. Commerce grew as the influx of people with court business arrived, requiring accommodations, transportation and food.

Of course, once there were criminals and convictions there needed to be a place to hold them. Since the courthouse dealt with all the issues in Burlington County, New Jersey's largest, rooms were at a premium in the small basement "gaol." Transporting prisoners to the larger jail in Burlington City was fraught with danger of interception and potential escape. Enter, Robert Mills, renowned Philadelphia architect.

The Burlington County Prison was built according to the most stringent and modern standards for a house of corrections known at the time. Mills went on to design the Washington Monument in Washington, D.C., and several buildings in the new capital. His legacy within the prison was in the solid construction and ease of management in a two-wing design, something incorporated into prisons for several years to come.

The stone walls and iron bars did not prohibit prisoners from seeking an early reprieve by their own devices:

> *$40 Reward for the return of two prisoners who escaped from the Burlington County Jail on January 31, 1819. Samuel Laning alias Hamlet, alias William Thompson, about 19 years of age, dark complexion, blue eyes and long curly hair; had on a blue rounabout jacket, grey*

Original Burlington County jail, 1810. This building has been restored and is a part of the County Parks and Recreation Department with regular tours. It was designed by Robert Mills, is the second oldest prison in the United States (next to Philadelphia's Eastern State Penitentiary) and was in regular use into the 1960s. *Photograph by author.*

> *pantaloons, common fur hat, about 5 feet 5 inches high. The other named Obadiah Read alias George Sommers about 26 years of age, light complexion, dark hair and large blue eyes; had on a velvet roundabout, blue cloth pantaloons, a fur hat nearly worn out, and a pair of old shoes. Forty dollars for both or twenty dollars for either. James Wilson, Jailor, Mount Holly.*

Montgomery Polehmus was one of the innkeepers who ran the Washington Hotel, at Water (Rancocas) and Main (High) Streets. This was one of the principal taverns in town, alongside the Three Tuns or Mill House Tavern on Mill and Pine. Polhemus's Inn had the advantage of being located a mere three doors from the courthouse, and he was very good at building on this. Several of the stage lines in town originated or were based at his hotel.

The public, recalling the ease by which the British had entered in 1776 and 1778 recognized that a militia needed to be maintained. For Mount Holly, being the center of county activity also meant sponsoring the local militia—the Mount Holly Guards. The militia, relics of the original colonial militia, were now controlled at the state level by the governor and formed into regiments at the county level. Each community, however, continued to raise and equip its own troops, usually of platoon or company size (twenty-five to one hundred members). These militia units became the seed of the initial state regiments sent in response to the Secession of the Southern states in

1861. They would also be called out by the sheriff of the county if needed for riot control or public assistance.

> *Regimental Orders Mount Holly May 15, 1819. The Muster and Inspection of the first Regiment of Militia in the Burlington Brigade will be at Mount Holly on Monday June 7, 1819. The several Corps composing the Regiment will assemble on parade at nine o'clock in the morning in front of the Court House. The Regiment will then be formed: the Mount Holly Guards taking post on the right—the Artillery in the centre—and the New Mills Volunteers on the right of the second Battalion. The Roll will be called at ten o'clock precisely. By order of Colonel Read. John Newbold, Adjutant.*[77]

Members of the community served in the War of 1812 and in the war with Mexico, though not in large numbers. For example, William M. Ewan served in Captain Joseph Yard's Company in the Mexican War. After his return from the scenes of his heroism, he was presented with a sword paid for by numerous citizens of Mount Holly and became involved in later debates regarding the value of war in solving the slavery problem.[78] However, the Mount Holly community was mostly focused on economics.

6.

Political, Economic and Agricultural Leadership

A. Shiras, Dentist, has recommenced the practice of his profession. Also at his store will be found a general assortment of dry goods, groceries, crockery, etc. Mount Holly, NJ

New store: Joseph C. Clark & Co. Having taken the store lately occupied by Edmund Burr, opposite the Friends' Meeting House, and two doors below Mr. Polhemus' Tavern inform their friends and the general public that they have an elegant assortment of dry goods, groceries, and the very best of liquors. Mount Holly.

Shoe Manufactory. Joshua Jones of Mount Holly takes this method of informing his friends and the public that he has removed from his old stand to the shop next door to William Chew (lately occupied by William Jobes as a Tailor's Shop) where he will make men's shoes, women's leather and morocco shoes, etc. Double coverlid and damask diaper weaving—also point work Bed Spreads—line work coverlids—double and figure work Carpeting—common diaper of various descriptions—flowered and common huckabuck [a type of coarse linen], *and fancy weaving in general, neatly executed at the Shop of Joseph H. Reeve, situated on the main road from Mount Holly to the Monmouth Court House, and within ¾ of a mile of Mount Holly.*

French Fire King, Mons Chaubert's Tapuyas Elixir, An instanteous cure for the Tooth Ache.—For sale at P. V. Coppuck's Drug and Medical Store, by the dozen or single bottle. Mount Holly.

Joseph Bennet informs his friends and the public that he continues to carry on the chair-making business at the dwelling house of his father, opposite the Tavern of Montgomery Polhemus, in Mount Holly, where Windsor and rush bottomed chairs may be had.[79]

— New Jersey Mirror

A Center of Trade

As New Jersey had been the "Crossroads of the American Revolution," so, by the turn of the nineteenth century, Mount Holly had become the "Crossroads of South Jersey." When trade began to focus on the growing city of Philadelphia, Mount Holly shifted its purpose to becoming a suburb of that expanding city. Shipping along the Rancocas evolved into a shuttle service, taking goods and people to Philadelphia,

Lumber mill on the Rancocas. *Courtesy Mount Holly Historical Society.*

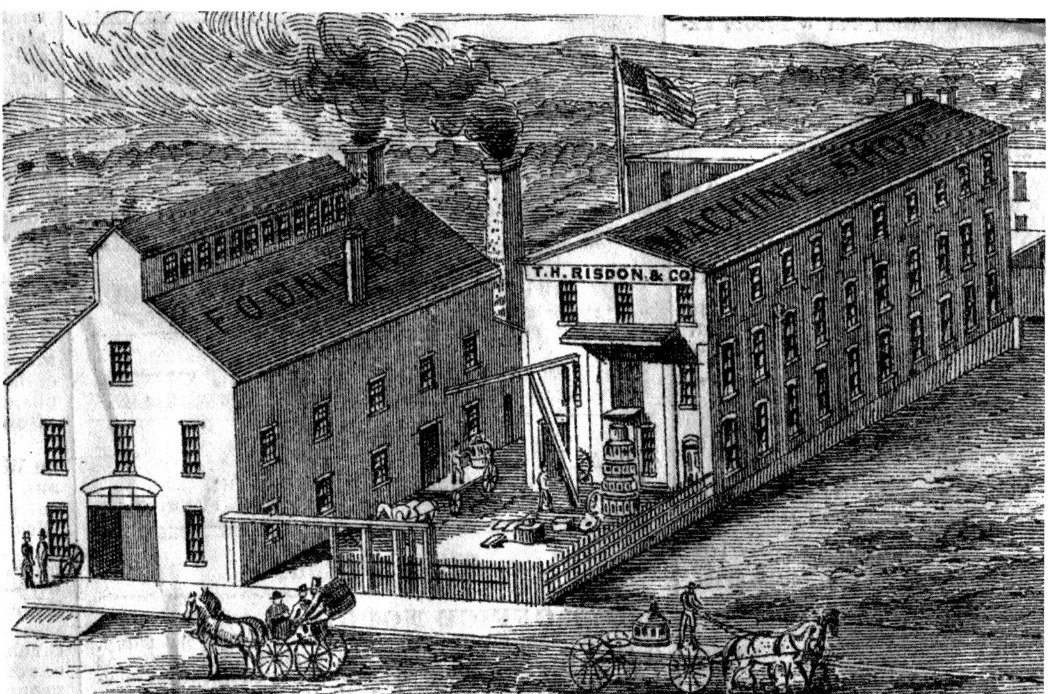

Illustration of Risdon Foundry, Mount Holly. *Cowgill Collection, Mount Holly Historical Society.*

where larger ships would take over for the trip to the Caribbean or Europe. Mills and manufactories, such as those found in Mount Holly, were able to manufacture goods and materials for export as well as for local use and a significant merchant and investor class evolved.

Production of lumber and agricultural products was being augmented by manufacture of steel and iron machinery and parts. Foundries produced wheels and gears for shipment to Europe and South America, sawmills continued their tasks of supplying construction needs in the area and countless small shops arose to supply the needs of the community. The worldwide influence of the products and materials produced in Mount Holly at that time may seem odd to us now, but it is only our own bias that causes us to believe that people in this day were isolated and ignorant of world markets, products and ideas.

Well-off farmers, the scions and leaders of the agricultural community, left the work to their children and retired to town. Many of the homes built along High Street and Mill Street in the early to middle nineteenth century were those of Scattergood, Risdon, Gaskill, Bispham, Dobbins, Hatkinson, Budd, Burr, Bryant, Cripps, Read, Reeves, Woolman and the like—families of the original settlers. No longer needed in the fields, they turned to town and county political and commercial enterprises benefiting the community. They became investors in rail and steamship companies and banks.

The Industrial Revolution was making its mark throughout the United States at this time. An increase in a cash-basis economy opened the door for a true middle class in town. Mount Holly, as the county seat, became the center for county activity, including the annual County Agricultural Fair, begun in 1847. The fair became a major attraction well into the early twentieth century, becoming one of the principal venues on the racing circuit for trotters and thoroughbreds.

Professionals and entrepreneurs from Philadelphia made Mount Holly their summer residence, and then their permanent residence once transportation to the city was reduced to an hour or so. Among these was Isaac Hazlehurst, who purchased most of the Cripps and Gaskill land, including the Mount. The Hazelhurst-Ashurst Estate on Garden and Branch Streets remains as a reminder of the large property and gardens known as Clover Hill. The balance of the property was sold off in 1948 to a developer who built the homes presently located near the mansion.[80]

New immigrants brought commercial success, such as Theodores Zurbrugg, a Swiss watchmaker, who opened a watch and clock shop in town and sought to develop land near King Street as a watch case factory. Rebuffed by the cost of land, he moved the factory to Riverside, where the company was very successful. The rising cost of land is an early indication of the significance of the location.

Justus Strawbridge clerked in a dry goods store in Mount Holly and later met William Clothier, resident of Mount Holly. Both entered into the dry goods business in Mount Holly and Haddonfield before moving their location to Philadelphia, continuing in the dry goods business and expanding to home and fashion. Together they formed

Trotters take the track at the Mount Holly Fairgrounds, circa 1890. *Courtesy Mount Holly Historical Society.*

Ashurst Estate (Clover Hill). This building was supposedly the offshoot of a summer cottage constructed by Isaac Hazlehurst and inherited by his daughter and son-in-law, the Ashursts. *Photograph by author.*

Mill and Main (High) Streets circa 1868–70. The Arcade was called the Black Horse Tavern when owned by William Davis (on the sign). Note the flagpole (later replaced by the fountain) and the spire of Trinity Church in the background. Businesses continued to shape and change the appearance of downtown as they built new buildings, changed old ones, and moved homes and houses around the town. Moving large and small houses is not a new concept, and teams of mules and oxen served where today we use diesel trucks. In 1904 Trinity Church was dismantled for its lumber. *Courtesy Mount Holly Historical Society.*

The notorious West End Hotel. In today's lingo, "What happens here, stays here." *Courtesy Mount Holly Historical Society.*

the regional firm of Strawbridge and Clothier, a multi-faceted department store, at one time becoming as large as New York's Macy's. Strawbridge's, the remnant of that partnership, was bought out by Macy's in 2006.

Others continued to expand the lumber and millwork businesses, farming supplies and commercial sales, transportation and communication, packing and canning. There is a very good recount of these folks in Henry Shinn's work and that of Zachariah Read. The area from High on either Washington or Water (Rancocas) Streets was filled with industry and commercial establishments.

COMMUNICATION AND COMMUTING

The operation of stagecoaches for transportation of passengers and freight was not new. England and most of Europe had the vehicles for centuries. As the need for communication with Philadelphia, Burlington and other cities grew, so did the need for stage lines. These were the equivalent of today's bus lines.

The journal of J.W. Erwin is very illustrative in that it shows that there was a continuous and regular interaction between the people of Philadelphia and the surrounding area as far away as Springfield (Jacksonville). With the advent of steamboats and the Camden-Amboy Railroad, travel time had been cut from a full

Center of town, showing Arcade Hotel and businesses at High Street and Washington. *Courtesy Mount Holly Historical Society.*

day to an hour. An entry from May 31, 1844: "Left Burlington this morning about ¼ of 8 and arrived in the city by ¼ past 9." It was an hour trip—not so great a difference from today:[81]

> *Mount Holly and Burlington Accommodation Stage (Old Line). Budd & Burr respectfully inform their friends and the public that they intend running a Stage daily throughout the season—leaving the Inns of Thomas Pearce, Joseph Hatkinson, Thomas Smith, and Montgomery Polhemus in Mount Holly every morning at 6:30 AM and arrive in Burlington to meet the Steamboats for Philadelphia and there await the arrival of the morning boats from Philadelphia and Trenton and return to Mount Holly in time to dine. The Stage will also run in the afternoon each day leaving the above-mentioned Inns at 1:30 PM and in Burlington await the arrival of the boats from Philadelphia and return immediately to Mount Holly. They propose running a four horse stage on Saturday, Sunday, and Monday of each week in order to accommodate all who wish to go. The driver is Curtis Shinn.*[82]

The trip to Philadelphia from Mount Holly took half a day, as it would seem from the schedule. At this point, that was superior to the full day or day and a half it took previously (depending on weather and road conditions) via the Cooper or Bristol Ferries. The season was spring through fall, travel in the winter being nigh impossible on the roads. Sleighs were used in that season for general travel as well as commercial

Carriage Repository in a later photograph. Personal carriages were stored here out of season, when most people would be using sleighs or not traveling at all. In addition, many people in town did not maintain carriages or even horses, but hired them as needed. In a sense, this would be the Hertz or Avis of the period. *Courtesy Cowgill Collection, Mount Holly Historical Society.*

transport. Ice in the river reduced the effectiveness of the steamboats of the day, and travelers resorted to the ferries or to staying at home.

J.W. Erwin's journal entry from January 22, 1846, stated:

> *Clear and very cold throughout the day and evening. The unusual sound of sleigh bells were constant today, and the vehicles dashed about with the speed which causes an exhilarating flow of blood in the spectator, and wakes a joyousness in those who are gliding swiftly along that is bodily and mentally refreshing. The sleighing was good, very good, and the most was made of it. Sleighs that have been quietly resting under shelter for a long time were pressed into service, and the speed of horses was unmercifully tried.*[83]

As the population of Mount Holly and the surrounding towns grew, so did the demand for transportation. People were no longer satisfied to stay on the farm and work seasonal jobs. They hired out work and hired on help for the farms and mills and traveled to Philadelphia for business. Competition was stiff for the traveler's dime (or quarter in this case):

> *Mount Holly & Burlington Accommodation Stage (Old Line).—Fare 25 Cents. William C. Budd of Mount Holly respectfully informs the public that he continues to run a daily Stage from Mount Holly to Burlington and has reduced the Fare to the low rate of 25 cents*

Madison Avenue circa 1875, from the Train Station to Lumberton, looking back at the mount in the distance. Wear your galoshes. *Courtesy Mount Holly Historical Society.*

> *for each passenger. The Stage will leave the Inns of Joseph Hatkinson and Thomas Smith every morning at 6 o'clock and arrive in Burlington to meet the Steamboats for Philadelphia and there await the arrival of the morning boats from Philadelphia and Trenton and return to Mount Holly in time to dine.*
>
> *Mount Holly and Burlington Steamboat Stage.—Fare 25 cents. Owing to the reduction in the prices of almost every article, and the scarcity of money, Jonathan Deacon of Mount Holly, has been induced to run a Stage from Mount Holly to Burlington to meet the Steamboats at the low rate of 25 cents for each passenger. The Stage will leave the Inn of Jonathan Deacon in Mount Holly every morning at 6 o'clock and arrive in Burlington in time to meet the Boats for Philadelphia. It will remain there until the arrival of the morning Boats from Philadelphia and Trenton and return to Mount Holly in time to dine.*[84]

There was regular traffic to the Jersey Shore, just like today. The trip was probably not much more debilitating than the current long lines of automobiles waiting on the Garden State Parkway, the Atlantic City Expressway and the access bridges and causeways on a Saturday morning in August. The Atlantic Ocean beaches were a draw for folks in the early 1800s as much as they are today. Mount Holly was positioned to take advantage of this traffic throughout the nineteenth and early twentieth centuries.

> *Philadelphia, Manahawkin & Elberson's Ferry Stage.—Andrew Elberson and Ezekiel Smith respectfully inform their friends and the public that they have commenced running a stage. To leave Arch Street Ferry at 2 o'clock, on every Monday and Friday afternoons, and thence to Moorestown, Mount Holly, New Mills, Cedar Bridge & Manahawkin, and arrive at Elberson's Ferry at 3 o'clock on Tuesday and Saturday afternoons, where Ladies and Gentlemen can be accommodated with Genteel Boarding and Lodging and conveyed across the Bay at any time to James Crammer's, Stephen Inman's, or any part of the seashore. Fares Through 2.50.*[85]

> *Manahawkin, Mount Holly and Burlington Stage.—Job F. Randolph proposes running a Stage from Manahawkin through Mount Holly to the City of Burlington to meet the Steamboats passing to and from Philadelphia. To commence the latter part of May 1821, leaving Manahawkin on the mornings of Wednesday and Saturday in time to meet the Steamboats at Burlington on the following mornings and leave Burlington on the afternoons of Sunday and Thursday and arrive at Manahawkin on the following afternoons in time to meet the stage for Tuckerton the same evening. Fare through 1.75.*[86]

As early as 1823 towns along the Rancocas were connected with Philadelphia by a steamer called the *Norristown*. Trips became semi-weekly when a group of Mount Holly leaders incorporated a company in 1824 to operate the *La Fayette* along the creek from Hilliard's Wharf to Philadelphia. To someone meandering the present-day Rancocas in a canoe or kayak, it is almost unfathomable that oceangoing vessels once traversed as far as Mount Holly. The creek was relatively deep through as far as Lumberton and shallow draft ships were in common use throughout the period.[87]

> *The Steamboat* Barclay, *Captain Peak, will commence running from Lumberton to Philadelphia on Tuesday morning, February 23, 1847. Leaving Lumberton at 6 o'clock and Long Bridge at half past 6 o'clock AM. Returning, will leave Philadelphia at 2 o'clock PM.*[88]

> *The steamers* Rancocas *and* Wave, *belonging to the Rancocas Steamboat Company, were purchased on February 23, 1855, by Daniel Miller of Philadelphia, probably for the Riverton Company. The* Barclay *was not sold. The* Barclay *has always done a large business and we have no doubt that with the increasing energies of the Company to accommodate the public, her number of passengers and amount of freight will be swelled to a corresponding and satisfactory extent.*[89]

> *A Steamboat Company having been organized to run a steamboat from Lumberton, in Burlington County, to Philadelphia and elsewhere, Barclay Haines was one of the leading spirits of the enterprise, and together with ten others of the prominent citizens of that community applied to the Legislature for a charter of incorporation, which was granted by that body in 1845, under the name and title of "The Rancocas Steamboat Company." They at once built the steamboat* Independence, *an iron hulled boat, the same that the Swedesboro'*

Illustrated Mount Holly wharf, in the *Herald. Courtesy Cowgill Collection, Mount Holly Historical Society.*

> *Steamboat Company afterwards purchased of them in 1846. Mount Holly, two miles distant, was connected therewith by stage; turnpikes were built to Hainesport from Mount Holly, Vincentown, Lumberton, &c.*[90]

Steamboat landings were plentiful by the mid-1800s and continuing until silt fill made the creek impossible to navigate. James Langstaff had a landing off Washington Street west of the bridge where he brought in the lumber to build his house.[91] Langstaff owned a large estate on High Street, built around 1830, which eventually became the home of the Mount Holly Library and Lyceum. Several property owners in town established personal landings along the creek, both behind King and Water Streets and along Pine Street and the Mills.

Shipping of goods and products occupied a large portion of the workforce during the heyday of the mid-1800s. The area of Monroe Park, along the creek where the baseball diamonds are today, was filled with warehouses and shops and wharfs for shipping. Another prime location in town was between Washington and King Streets, where the municipal parking lot is today. Additional shipping commenced at the Hainesport docks near the Long Bridge, where boats from Lumberton met those from Shrevesville and Mount Holly. Drawings from J.C. Cowgill's collection illustrate how the wharfs appeared.

Boat building took place on the creek in various locations, including at the dock of Isaac Hazelhurst near King Street (about the rear of the current Lippincott Supply). Isaac turned the business over to Samuel and Isaac Haines in 1859. Henry Shinn notes

Photo of riverboat on creek. This appears to be at the location of the railroad bridge over the Rancocas on the Mount Holly-Camden line at Hainesport. It illustrates the size of ships that plied the creek. *Courtesy Mount Holly Historical Society.*

Mount Holly and Burlington Railroad Station at Madison Avenue, late 1800s. This is now a restaurant. *Courtesy Burlington County Library.*

the last vessel produced at that facility was in 1888, the launching of which he attended with his father.[92]

The Camden and Burlington County Rail Line (C&BC) was conceived shortly after the successful opening of the Camden and Amboy Rail Road, which followed a route originating in Perth Amboy, traveling along the river from Bordentown, through Burlington City, to Camden in 1836. From there passengers could board ferries to Philadelphia or ships to points farther south. It became the alternate to travel by sea between New York and Philadelphia.

A second railroad, the Burlington and Mount Holly Railroad and Transportation Company, was incorporated in 1836, but construction was delayed by the financial panic of 1837, and the line was not completed until the late 1840s. The two railroads crossed in East Burlington. In the 1890s, the Pennsylvania Railroad used the Burlington and Mount Holly tracks to experiment with electric operation, but this service was discontinued after the electrical powerhouse in Mount Holly burned. The Burlington and Mount Holly line was abandoned in 1927, but the Camden and Amboy line remains in use, though only by Conrail freight trains.[93]

Frank Kozempel provides an interesting history from the Pennsylvania Railroad's perspective:

> *Several segments of the latter day C.&B.C. predate the construction of its mainline. Following completion of New Jersey's first railroad, The Camden and Amboy (C.&A.) in 1834 interest developed to access the interior of Burlington County. Mount Holly, the county seat, seven miles east of the C.&A. mainline was an obvious choice. The Burlington and Mount Holly Railroad and Transportation Company was incorporated February 11, 1848 to construct this line. The original station was located on Grant Street near the current County Court Complex. In 1863, the line was extended from Mount Holly to Pemberton. The name of the original railroad was changed by incorporation to the Burlington County Railroad Company on July 4, 1863.*[94]

The burning of the electric powerhouse in Mount Holly and the need to rebuild provided an impetus for the construction of a trolley line between Mount Holly and Burlington. The local Mount Holly Street Railway Company was acquired by the Camden and Suburban and reorganized as the Burlington County Traction Company. By 1904 tracks were in place from Camden to Burlington by way of Mount Holly. The Traction Company suffered several years of economic deficits and equipment problems, and agreed to sell its equipment and franchises to the Public Service Transportation Corporation.[95]

As noted, Strawbridge and Clothier was a prominent department store in Philadelphia and the area, akin to Macy's in New York. Many employees continued to live in Mount Holly and commuted to Philadelphia and the surrounding area to their work. In fact, many physicians, lawyers and other professionals maintained offices in Philadelphia while living in Mount Holly.

Madison Hotel at corner of Washington and Madison Avenues. The railroad roundhouse was located to the rear of this building. The main line of the Camden and Mount Holly Railroad ran to this junction at Madison and Washington. *Courtesy Cowgill Collection, Mount Holly Historical Society.*

"The Corner" at Brainerd and Buttonwood, with the "four-room school," as it was called (right), and the Academy building (left). This was the original location of the first Mount Holly High School as well. *Courtesy Mount Holly Historical Society.*

Mount Nebo Church Building (old "colored" school), now the meeting place for a large and diverse congregation. *Photograph by author.*

EDUCATION

Another effect of the growth of the town during this period was the growth of formal schooling. As noted earlier, schooling up until the mid-nineteenth century was somewhat informal and based on practical matters, the exceptions being those children of the well-to-do who attended preparatory schools for college. By 1850–60, Mount Holly had several prominent and well-respected schools.

The Mount Holly Academy commenced operations in 1818, under the tutelage of William Mann and had already been in operation for many years, as had numerous smaller and specialized private schools.

> *Examination. Notice to the public and particularly the parents of the pupils of the Mount Holly Academy, that a public examination will take place on December 2, 1818 at the Academy at 9 AM after which a 2 week vacation will be given.*[96]
>
> *William Mann of Mount Holly takes this method to inform the public that he is willing to receive pupils to board with him—and the terms of tuition and board will be thirty dollars per quarter, for the youth that are under 14. The Mount Holly Academy will open April 5, 1819.*[97]

William Aaron founded the well-respected Treemount School in Pennsylvania before being forced by economic misfortune to relocate to Mount Holly, taking a position as minister of the First Baptist Church.

> *Becoming involved in the financial crisis of 1857, through endorsements for a friend who failed for a large amount, Mr. Aaron gave up to his creditors; abandoned the pleasant home which his taste and enterprise had beautified and adorned, and where he had no doubt anticipated passing the remainder of his days; and removing to Mt. Holly, accepted a call to the Pastorship of the Baptist Church—a position he retained till his death.*[98]

In September 1857, Mr. Aaron and his son Charles E. Aaron opened the Mount Holly Institute on Brainerd Street, affiliated with the Baptist Church. The facility occupied an area that has become known for the proliferation of seats of learning throughout the history of the town—the corners of Buttonwood and Brainerd Streets.

Samuel Miller founded the West Jersey Collegiate Institute in a frame building near where Rancocas Valley Regional High School is today. Many of his graduates went on to further education at Princeton, the University of Pennsylvania, Yale and other places of higher learning. The institute is mentioned in articles and notes from around the region and the country, and was a well-respected boarding school for young men.[99]

Schools expressly for the black community started early in the 1840s. A small school was built around 1847 and was in use until the fall of 1873.[100] The general position was to segregate the races in education as in other pursuits, even in the "enlightened" North. Considering 1847 was the same year three escaped slaves were remanded to their owner by the Burlington Court, separation of education is not a surprise.

In 1874 a new school was built off of West Washington Street in a building now occupied by the Mount Nebo Church. That the new school continued the practice of separation of the races, well after the bloodiest war in American history served to remove slavery as an option in America, speaks volumes about public attitude. The school was in use until the 1950s when racial segregation in schools was outlawed.

7.

A Wound That Will Not Heal

These are the people by whose labor the other inhabitants are in a great measure supported, and many of them in the luxuries of life. These are the people who have made no agreement to serve us, and who have not forfeited their liberty that we know of. These are the souls for whom Christ died, and for our conduct towards them we must answer before Him who is no respecter of persons. They who know the only true God, and Jesus Christ whom he hath sent, and are thus acquainted with the merciful, benevolent, gospel spirit, will therein perceive that the indignation of God is kindled against oppression and cruelty, and in beholding the great distress of so numerous a people will find cause for mourning.

—John Woolman, 1753[101]

Abolitionists, the Underground Railroad and Slave Catchers

Quakers held a high place for abolition. Many of the principal agents offering support and protection to escaped slaves were Quakers. To a great extent, the writings of John Woolman and the preaching of Josiah White, both of Mount Holly, played a crucial role in establishing this philosophy among their brethren.

Slavery was the great conundrum in American politics, dating from the time of the Declaration of Independence. Several decisions in the U.S. Supreme Court gave credence to the ownership rights of slaveholders. While states like New Jersey had begun to eliminate slave trade and slave ownership in the early 1800s, federal law required that local courts impound and return the rightful property of the slave owner. Personified by Lawyer Marks and Tom Loker in *Uncle Tom's Cabin*, slave catchers were employed to roam the countryside searching for runaways and returning them to the plantation for a fee. It would seem that both hunters and hunted were frequent visitors to Mount Holly.

An early community located about a mile from the center of Mount Holly is referred to as Timbuctoo, located off of present-day Rancocas Road. Many sections of Mount Holly had adopted colorful names, such as Turpentine, Santa Domingo and Sand Hill.

Timbuctoo was different in that it was a community of what were termed free blacks, a community of color. Self-sustaining for the most part, it consisted of individuals who owned their own property, farmed and worked various skilled trades in the area near the Rancocas in what is now Westampton Township. Many were employed locally in the mills and farms, and as house servants for the well to do. Some were also escaped slaves.

The Underground Railroad passed through and by Mount Holly from inception. Composed of three different routes, from Eastern Shore Maryland through Delaware, Philadelphia and New Jersey, the ultimate goal was Upstate New York and Canada.[102] In Mount Holly, the only building that claims to have been a part of this is the old Hazlehurst-Ashurst Mansion, and its role is not clear. For the most part, fugitive slaves were provided assistance in communities like Timbuctoo. The general white population of Mount Holly was not so completely in favor of abolition as to serve as a safe haven.

> *In Timbuctoo, near Mount Holly, on Friday last, HEZEKIAH HALL, (colored) aged about 60 years. The deceased, in early life, was a slave, and belonged to Charles Carroll, of Carrollton. He escaped from bondage in the year 1814. He settled in our midst about the year 1824, since which time he has resided here. He was regarded by every one(sic) as a man of unblemished character, and his truly upright walk and Christian deportment commanded the highest respect. His remains were followed to the grave on Sunday last by a very large concourse of friends and neighbors.*[103]

> Mount Holly Herald—*Fall, 1847*[104]
> *Considerable excitement was created in our community on Wednesday last in consequence of the arrest of three colored persons residing at Timbuctoo, named Commodore Chase, Aaron Chase, and Elizabeth Brooks (brothers and sister) by a person from Cecil County Maryland, who claims them as his slaves.*

The three were brought before Judge Haywood at Mount Holly and a jury returned a verdict in favor of the claimant. There was a large crowd of black citizens from Timbuctoo attending and milling around the courthouse throughout the day. The three captives "rushed upon the crowd and attempted to escape." The judge called on the local National Guard, who provided security and assistance to the sheriff in moving the prisoners through the crowd to the jail and patrolled the streets throughout the night. The opinion of the press was that the sheriff and the others had done their duty well.

As Professor Giles Wright states, life as a black person in New Jersey was dangerous and uncertain.[105] It should be of no surprise that slave catchers and kidnappers would meet group resistance. The September 10, 1850 issue of the *New Jersey Mirror* noted:

> *The passage of the fugitive slave law and the results attending it, has caused the most intense excitement among the numerous colored persons residing in the vicinity of Mount*

> *Holly. We do not wonder that this should be the case. Those residing at the settlements around us have held many consultations and we are quite sure that any person going among them for the purpose of making an arrest would meet with a reception that would not be at all agreeable.*

Not all slave catchers were successful. The importance of these independent black communities in that regard cannot be understated. Providing refuge for all, and a central community for support, they became an important link in what would come to be called the Underground Railroad.

The following article appeared in the *Mirror* only two months later:

> *At the colored church in Burlington (Bethlehem AME), on Sunday evening week, a number of negroes, suspecting a black man in the crowd to be acting as a spy for slave holders, made an attack on him. He was badly stabbed, and, escaping from the church, took refuge in a carpenter's shop, into which he got by breaking a window. He here defended himself with an axe. The blacks everywhere are very much alarmed in reference to the provisions of the fugitive slave law, and it is not at all surprising that they should be excited in the highest degree when they have suspicions that a spy is hovering around their camp. But we think their better policy would be to remain as quiet as possible.*[106]

The Battle in the Swamp took place near Timbuctoo in 1851. A slave catcher entered the village with several citizens of Mount Holly to capture Perry Simmons, lately escaped from the South. Local residents took up arms to repel him and several people were injured. Not much is known about this engagement as yet, but Mr. Simmons was never captured.[107]

> *Perry Simmons, the colored man, whose attempted arrest as a fugitive slave, on two occasions, created considerable excitement in our neighborhood, died in Timbuctoo, a week or two ago. Perry had not been well since the last attempt to capture him, in consequence of taking a severe cold on that freezing night. It will be recollected that he was forced to fly suddenly from his bedroom to the garret, where he was obliged to remain till morning, suffering severely from the cold. Perry is at last beyond the reach of his Southern master.*[108]

All of this said, the work of the underground was rightly covert in a state where an elected Senator claimed that the difficulty in the state was "not about surrendering fugitive slaves to their legal masters but rather how to get rid of those worthless slaves which the South suffer to escape into our territory, and remain there to the annoyance of our people."[109] The tensions between black and white were palpable, even in a "tolerant" community in the North.

Mount Holly's AME church congregations can draw at least some of their history from the residents of this village of Timbuctoo. This enclave of between one and two hundred residents embraced the AME philosophy in the 1850s with the establishment of the Zion Wesley AME Church. By 1904 there were three AME churches in the area, with the incorporation of Mount Olive AME Church in 1874 by "King" David Parker and others.

The word "African" means that the church was organized by people of African descent and heritage. The church's roots lie in the family of Methodist churches, hence "Methodist" in the title. Episcopal refers to the form of government under which the church operates.[110]

Abductions and wrongful captures of former slaves continued, despite the efforts of local free blacks to stem the tide. Current concern about child-abduction is nothing new. The *New Jersey Mirror* (March 6, 1856) contains the story of a young boy by the name of Anderson, who lived with his free family. He was befriended by a man from Hainesport, who promised him work at his father's milk business in West Philadelphia. The boy and man negotiated terms, he agreed to the employment and went with the man to Philadelphia. But they continued to Baltimore, where the man attempted to sell the boy for $500. The boy ran to the Quakers there, telling them he was not a slave, but was taken from his family in Mount Holly. The phony slave owner was arrested and imprisoned; the Friends took care of the boy and returned him to his parents.[111]

An interesting note is that Timbuctoo is often recalled in oral histories as the site of "camp meetings" during the nineteenth and early twentieth centuries. Many older residents remember the noisy and boisterous crowds of blacks and whites gathering to hear the preachers and singing. The rich heritage is seen today in the broad appeal of the church in the community and the many services and supports it provides to members and non-members alike; and, occasionally, there are still camp meetings.

THE WAR OF THE REBELLION

February 15, 1855—A debate will take place at the Lyceum, Mount Holly, on Monday evening February 19, 1855, between William M. Ewan and Joseph Allinson on the question: "Is War justifiable under any circumstances." Mr. Ewan, affirmative. Mr. Allinson, negative. Admission 6½ cents.

March 8, 1855—The ladies and public are invited to attend a Debate between W.M. Ewan and J. Allinson at Concert Hall, Mount Holly on Monday evening March 12, 1855 on the question: "Is war justifiable under any circumstances." Mr. Ewan will have his sword. Ladies free. Gentlemen 10 cents.

Like its neighboring towns, Mount Holly was the scene of numerous debates as to the validity of slavery, the viability of controlling it in the new territories as they became states of the union, and the viability of keeping that union together by war. New Jersey did not vote for Abe Lincoln in 1860, and his inauguration train was whisked through the state to avoid confrontation and conflict. Most citizens of New Jersey, and Mount Holly, were not interested in fighting a war to free slaves. However, once the Southern states seceded, and Lincoln called for troops to protect the integrity of the Union, New Jersey responded quickly.

Governor Olden sent the four principal New Jersey Guard regiments (First, Second, Third and Fourth) to Washington in time to participate in the First Battle of Bull Run in July 1861. Members of Mount Holly's home guard were mostly part of the Third and Fourth Regiments in the overall scheme of the army, and part of General Phil Kearny's Jersey Brigade. Later in the war many area residents became part of the Thirty-fourth New Jersey Volunteers. Quakers once again urged a peaceful solution and sought to keep their members out of the enlistments. Many went willingly, and many did serve once called by the draft.

> *A number of young men, former residents of this county, were in the battle of Ball's Bluff. George Groom, son of Edward Groom of this town (Mount Holly), escaped from the rebels by swimming the river. Messrs. Elwood and Willard, two young men who taught school here, a year or two since, the former at the Mount Holly Institute, and the latter at Unionville, were in the engagement. Mr. Elwood has been heard from by his friends, but Mr. Willard, it is thought, was among the slain or is a prisoner.*[112]

News from the front was intermittent and often depended on the reporters in the field for accuracy. Newspapers would post lists of the wounded, dead and missing on their boards. There were no news conferences announcing the latest affairs of the army. The advent of television has made battlefield reporting so commonplace today that we forget it might have taken weeks or months for news to arrive from distant skirmishes.

> *A letter was received in this town, on Monday, from Captain William Nippins, dated Richmond, July 1st, in which he sends us the list of killed and wounded in his company. Fifty-one of his company are prisoners, in the Tobacco warehouse* [Libby Prison] *Richmond. About 25 officers and 300 privates of the Fourth regiment, were taken prisoners and marched to Richmond. These prisoners will doubtless be released in a short time. We had hoped that Capt. Nippins would send home the names of all of his company who were taken prisoners. It would be a matter of much interest to their friends here to see their names published, announcing them safe and uninjured, although prisoners among the rebels.*[113]

Often the only remembrance of a loved one was what are referred to as Cartes de Visit—photographs taken upon enlisting or before leaving. Swaim's Photography Studios in Mount Holly took this photo of local resident Samuel Read, who served as quartermaster for the First New Jersey Volunteers.

Families would often know nothing of a loved one's fate until long after a battle in which his unit participated. Families in Mount Holly felt part of the front, concerned when Lee's army encroached into Pennsylvania in July of 1863 and cheered when he was repulsed by Meade. Reading of the engagements and results much the same way we followed reports from World War II and Korea, they held a variety of opinions. In fact, in the 1864 national election, while the *New Jersey Mirror*, the *Mount Holly Herald* and other papers campaigned for Lincoln-Johnson, New Jersey's voters approved Democrat and former General George McClellan, who wanted to negotiate with the South for peace. The following was recorded in the *Mirror*:

Swaim's Photographic Studios, Mount Holly. *Courtesy Mount Holly Historical Society collection.* Inset: Samuel Read, Quartermaster, First New Jersey Regiment, carte de visit done at Swaim's in 1861 [stamped on reverse]. *Courtesy New Jersey Archives, Trenton.*

> *In recording the death of the youthful defenders of our country, in her direful contest with the aroused spirit of slavery, it is a pleasing reflection to know, in the midst of our sorrow, that they died, as the generous and brave desire to die, in the full performance of duty to their country and their God. So fell the maimed and heroic Capt. Richard L.R. Shreve, on the 6th of May, in the battle of the Wilderness, while leading his company in a charge upon the enemy. Although reared in the peaceful doctrines of the Society of Friends, he was the youngest of four patriotic brothers that obeyed the summons of the nation, and marched to the deliverance of our country from the ruthful control of a barbarous system of outrage and wrong. Two have already died that our country might live, and two yet remain with arms in their hands, doing battle for justice and right.*[114]

At the end of the war the families and townspeople faced the return of soldiers who had experiences most would never forget. An association of veterans called the Grand Army of the Republic (GAR) established posts throughout the northern United States. In Mount Holly the GAR post was established by twenty-five veterans.[115] They sought to assist each other in getting back into civilian life, and many suffered from what we would now know as post-traumatic stress; they drank, left home and generally had difficulty fitting back into society. Often, their fellow veterans at the post were the only ones who understood.

As with any war, the Civil War left a legacy far beyond that intended by those who initiated and waged it. The soldiers returning to Mount Holly, Shrevesville, Lumberton, Medford and Pemberton brought greater knowledge of worldly affairs. Many had never been more than a few miles from home and now had traveled thousands of miles, witnessing a variety of cultures and ideas. Many turned their experience into a personal pride in accomplishment and brought their sense of duty to their jobs in the industrial expansion.

8.

The Gilded Age

Gardens and Debutantes

Following the Civil War, Mount Holly returned to its former role as economic and agricultural center for the county. New industries were spawned by the effects of the war, including mass production of canned fruits, vegetables and meats, shipping of produce to Philadelphia terminals and the revitalization of the cotton-based textile industry. Semple's thread company took off, producing what was noted to be the finest cotton thread and yarn available for the textile industry.

Several local industrialists, including Hezekiah B. Smith of Smithville and Samuel Risdon, started production facilities for machinery, tools and even bicycles. Samuel Semple marketed his brand of cotton thread to the world, making Mount Holly world-renowned in the field, and becoming rich in the process.[116]

The Mount Holly Agricultural Fair took on increased recognition and regional importance, and the railroad brought people into town from afar. Alexander Graham Bell's invention, exhibited at the 1876 Centennial Exhibition in Philadelphia, came to town in 1878. The two crude phones connected the Washington House with the fairgrounds and were an attraction worth paying a few cents to try. By 1883 there were a full twenty-five subscribers to the new telephone service.[117]

Going to the fair is described curiously in testimony at a trial in 1893:

> *Lizzie and Wesley came on from Brooklyn to spend the Fourth of July; they arrived on Saturday; on Thursday…we all went to the fair…and twice during the day we went to the stand where Wesley was working and each time he gave Lizzie fifty cents; we then went to the flying swing and took a ride; we were with Ollie Broom and Annie Rossell and some young fellows we knew from Burlington; we afterwards went over to the beer bar under the grand stand and took a seat outside; one of the fellows went in and brought out five glasses of beer.*[118]

The fairgrounds, located where the Acme at Fairgrounds Plaza is now, had quite the grandstand. The overall grounds included the area now occupied by the tract of

Fairgrounds and the crowd on the Midway. The tents were filled with games of chance and beer vendors, much the same as today's county fairs. *Courtesy Mount Holly Historical Society.*

Entertainment included evening concerts in town and at the fairgrounds by famous entertainers as well as such local talent as the Liberty Zouave Band and Mount Holly Cornet Band. *Courtesy Cowgill Collection, Mount Holly Historical Society.*

Fairgrounds Grandstand. *Courtesy Mount Holly Historical Society.*

The Good Old Game, 1865. The Mount Holly Baseball Club functioned in various forms from after the Civil War to the mid-1940s. Inset: Scores posted in the *Mount Holly Herald*, 1866. Note that the Mount Holly Baseball Club beat the Alvin Baseball Club of Philadelphia, 23 to 22. *Courtesy Cowgill Collection, Mount Holly Historical Society.*

homes along Woodpecker Lane. A horse track was part of the facility, and races were run for large purses, drawing regional and national contenders.

Local sports competition blossomed with organized baseball teams. That's right, there were pick-up teams playing the game as early as the American Revolution and by the mid-nineteenth century the sport was played in almost every town. During the Civil War baseball between platoons and companies was regularly reported, and the residents of prisoner-of-war camps regularly played games with prisoners versus guards.

After the war soldiers brought the lure of the game home with them. Mount Holly's baseball club had a great reputation and good players. They would often play teams from Philadelphia and Camden. The best players had to have tough hands—literally, there were no gloves.

WEALTH AND CAPITAL

It would be hard to imagine today, walking through the town, that almost every inch of available space not occupied by a home or business was occupied by a factory. The area bounded by Washington, Grant and King Streets was occupied by a carpet factory, a major cannery, lumber yards, shipbuilding facilities and a foundry.

Samuel Semple & Sons was located in Shrevesville about the time H.B. Smith bought the site. The company moved into its new, larger plant at the corner of King and Washington streets in 1867, and manufactured a high-grade cotton thread, which was awarded medals at the Centennial Exposition in Philadelphia in 1876. The business passed out of the control of the Semple family in about 1886 and the plant was converted into a carpet factory that was destroyed by fire in 1896.[119]

Political intrigue, scandalous behavior, cash and stock manipulation, colorful antics and industrial success would together make a perfect book or film. These do not refer to some modern-day elected official or entertainer, but to Hezekiah B. Smith, of Smithville. H.B. was notorious from the day he entered town to pick up Shrevesville's assets at a bargain. This was the old Parker operation two miles outside of town, and H.B. wanted to use it as his visionary and self-contained industrial village—utopia on the Rancocas?

H.B. came in with guns blazing and made a real impression on the townspeople of Mount Holly, providing work and an outlet for local goods and services. He set up the H.B. Smith and Company foundry and factory, producing assorted metal and machine parts and molding. Several of his employees went on to found their own operations, such as William Kelly, of Kelly-Springfield, who invented the pneumatic tire. At the time of his death H.B. personally held several patents, including one in 1889 for a steam-powered tricycle.[120]

The Smithville works produced a number of bicycle styles, including the "Star." The design was unique for the period in that it featured the rear wheel being far larger than the front wheel. The bicycle was entered into many national and international competitions and was a huge moneymaker.

The works also produced the most unusual feature of late nineteenth-century New Jersey: the Bicycle Railroad. The purpose was to provide a means for workers

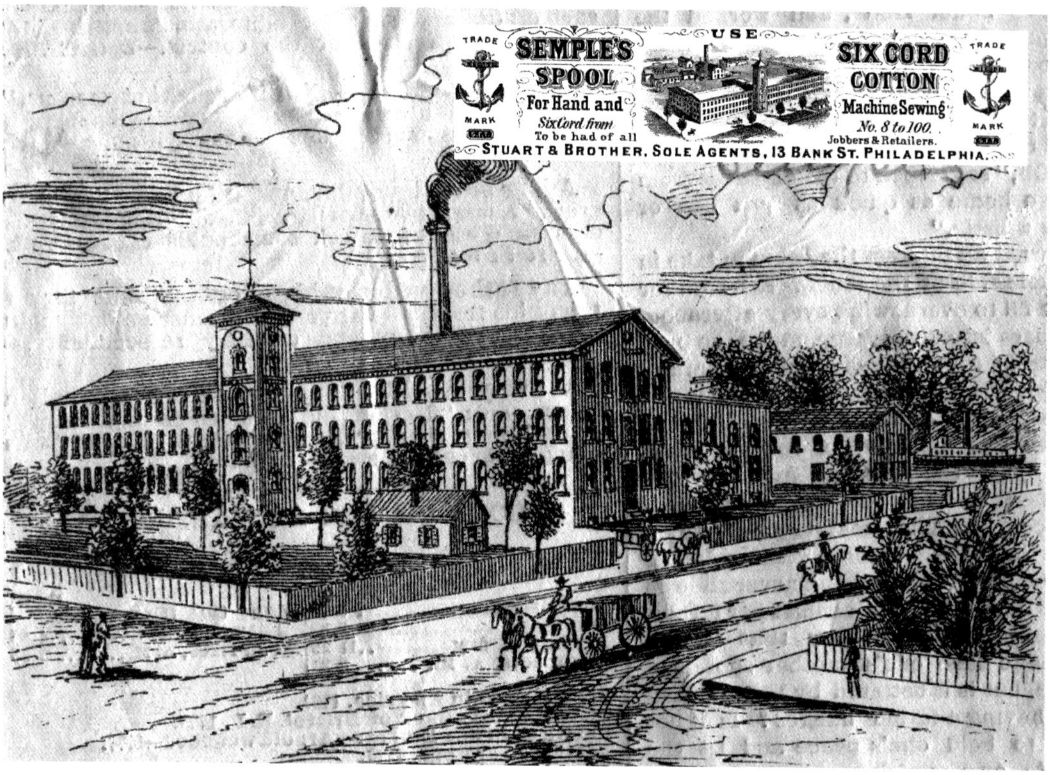

Illustration of the Semple and Sons Thread factory at Washington and King Streets. The size of the Semple Factory shows the extent the business had expanded, and the general state of business in Mount Holly as well. Inset: Ad for Semple and Sons Thread. *Courtesy Cowgill Collection, Mount Holly Historical Society.*

John Dobbins wrangling the Moose Cart. H.B. Smith's eccentricity was personified in his insistence on using the moose to pull his cart in local parades. *Courtesy Mount Holly Historical Society.*

in Mount Holly to get to their jobs in Smithville. It only lasted a couple of years because of impracticality. An excellent discussion of this is found in Smith and Winzinger and in Bolger.

H.B. brought economic growth to Smithville and Mount Holly. He also brought bigamy, political intrigue and social shenanigans unlike any seen since. His personal "zoo" included at least one moose, which he harnessed to a cart to draw attention for his political campaigns (he served in congress for one term). In a day and age when the circus arrived in town with a full-blown parade from the train to the fair grounds, H.B.'s ambling moose cart would have generated a similar parade of youngsters and others and was noted to have created quite a scene.

AN ERA OF SOCIAL COMPETITION

As personal wealth resulted in greater leisure time, families began building comfortable summer retreats and year-round homes for themselves. The Ashursts maintained extensive gardens at Clover Hill.

The Nathan Dunn property, called the Chinese Cottage because of his status in the China Trade, was used by Mr. Dunn as a summer residence in the early part of the nineteenth century. Now Sacred Heart Church and Parish Center, the extensive gardens held many exotic trees and shrubs imported from the Orient. Located at the front of the property are two beautiful Japanese maples, possibly the last remnants of the famous Dunn garden.[121]

The Levis family was the first to own the Chinese Cottage after Dunn's sisters both passed on. What once started out as Nathan Dunn's garden, consisting of twenty-five acres in the 1830s, eventually evolved into a lavish garden known to many in town and the surrounding area as Levis Garden. The Dunn property, which extended down to what is now known as Levis Drive, was covered with plants that had been brought from China as part of Dunn's business as tea and silk importer. When the Franklin B. Levis family bought the property in 1881, it was full of lovely exotic plants, which the Levises continued to cultivate.[122]

The property was sold in 1913 to the John and Elizabeth Johnson. In the social columns of the *New Jersey Mirror*, time and again there was mention of the parties that were given at the Johnsons' that continued using the estate's name of "Dunnmore" originally given by the Levis. One common description given for both families' parties is about the exotic plants and cut flowers, more than likely from the property or the conservatory, used to adorn the rooms.

At some point, most likely when the Levises left Dunnmore, some of the adjoining property was sold. This is where Edward H. Levis, the middle son, located his home. Moving farther down the street, he continued with the garden that Dunn had started. This garden became a highlight for Mount Holly. Families from all over the area, as far away as Delaware, would come to visit his garden, especially in the spring when all the bulbs bloom. Many of the residents would have photographs taken of their children or weddings taken there. It was said that it

Greenhouses at the rear of the Ashurst Estate, circa 1880. Note the bicycles, probably manufactured just down the road at the H.B. Smith factory in Smithville. The Gardens behind this home were well known and justly famous, though not so famous as those behind the Edward Levis home on High Street. *Courtesy Mount Holly Historical Society.*

was rivaled Longwood Gardens as a place to visit in the Delaware Valley. Mr. Levis bequeathed the garden to Mount Holly when he died but unfortunately the costs of upkeep became too high. The property now houses a school that was built in the early 1960s.[123]

Though Mount Holly retained much of its industrial flavor, the upper end of High Street and parts of Washington Street leading out of town became fashionable residential areas. Broad, Union and Ridgway Streets offered a reprieve from the bustle (and dirt) of the downtown. Most of life was spent in entertaining, visiting or attending concerts. Almost every home had formal gardens by the end of the nineteenth century, some including full-sized tennis courts. The well-to-do mingled with the lower classes only when their servants couldn't perform the errand.

The Concert Hall Association (see, another association) was established in 1875 and the town finally had a permanent location expressly for theater and entertainment. Known as the Opera House, it was the scene of many plays, performances, traveling theater troupes and minstrel shows. It was the variety show of its day and a precursor to vaudeville. It rivaled Philadelphia, with plays brought from the Walnut Street Theater in that town to be performed for the local populace and with the presence of such period attractions as General Tom Thumb (of Barnum's circus fame), Blind Tom and Eddie Foy.[124]

The Nathan Dunn Chinese Cottage (today's Sacred Heart parish house). Eventually became part of the Franklin Levis estate (father of Edward). *Photograph by author.*

As for town historians, Joseph Cowgill emerges as an interesting and sanguine character. His passion for local history helped guide this writer and countless others before. Joseph was a collector of memorabilia. His scrapbook provides a vast array of detailed information about the town during his lifetime and before, and diverse information, both funny and sad. His early pages belie the work of a youth (about fifteen to nineteen years of age) with collections of firehouse "trading cards" and pictures of scantily clad female "entertainers," which would have been utterly reprehensible for that prim period.

Much of what we know about Mount Holly from 1840 to 1900 is located somewhere in his scrapbook. A member of the Relief Fire Company and operating the family dry goods store, he shows the modern reader what the life of the middle class was like in the late nineteenth century. From the diversity of his collection, we can make certain assumptions about the focus and activity of the average person in Mount Holly at that time.

Envision downtown Mount Holly: the station, the stores, the shops and all the various activities. In the crowds would be prominent socialites (the sisters Budd and Kelly would be among them) as would the descendants of those entrepreneurs who made their riches in the early part of the nineteenth century. Merchants in their aprons and galoshes mingled on the sidewalk with well-dressed children returning home from

Levis Gardens. The Edward Levis house is the current Perenchief funeral parlor and some features of the old gardens can still be seen during annual garden tours, including a chestnut estimated at two hundred years of age. *Courtesy Mount Holly Master Gardeners and Mount Holly Historical Society.*

one or another of the schools in town. Black laborers and servants scurried about, being appropriately deferent to the Irish and Italian workers who were heading in and out of the Arcade, Mill or West End Hotels, while quietly attending to their own affairs and assets. Street urchins, as dusty and grimy as any in New York or London, traipse through the shops and alleys while store clerks swat at them in the belief they can only be looking to steal an apple or a candy stick. Carriages rumble through High Street and Mill Street (or slip and slide, depending on the weather) and horse droppings and various garbage combine to season the air with a multitude of odors. An early automobile, probably a Ford Model S, toots its way through town drawing the wonderment and occasional scorn of the onlookers, frightening the horses in an abominably uncivilized manner.

WOMEN HAVE A ROLE, TOO, YOU KNOW

For the longest time (actually, since they arrived in Mount Holly), women have played crucial roles in the management and operation of business, farming and

Cowgill's Dry Goods Store on High Street (Main), with Cowgill sitting on a box of *Silver Star Baking Soda* in the center. *Courtesy Cowgill Collection, Mount Holly Historical Society.*

cultural affairs. Women managed the daily operations of farmsteads, households and often the finances of the family. Women formed the backbone of social interaction and set the standards for interpersonal relationships. Still, the census of New Jersey in 1774 lists only four women in all of Northampton Township.[125] This census seeks to establish ratable, taxable property and goods. It is clear that women were not commonly the owners of property and, in many ways, were actually considered "chattel" themselves. Sarah Dawson, Annah Leeds, Elizabeth Southwick and Elizabeth Hatkinson were considered landowners for various reasons, but they were the exception. Elderly women and those "past the age of bearing children" were noted landholders, as were widows until they remarried.

The date when property ownership began to shift to include the average woman in American society is debated, but I believe that point came when the medical profession "discovered" what midwives and practitioners of herbal and natural medicine had known for centuries—how to reduce the incidence of death of the mother as a result of childbirth. When the natural and necessary phenomenon of bearing children was no longer the most common cause of death for women, they could no longer be

High Street Parade with the fire companies and the Julius Kleingunther New Year's Association of Philadelphia. This was an early "comic" association affiliated with the Philadelphia Mummers parade. Cowgill notes that this organization provided a twenty-five-piece band and almost 150 marchers and performers. *Courtesy Cowgill Collection, Mount Holly Historical Society.*

viewed as risky property holders. Of course, social change occurs ever so slowly, and full acceptance of roles for women in "men's" affairs remains elusive even today.

Throughout history, women have demonstrated the capacity to tackle complex political and governmental issues alongside men. Queens had long proven that they could be the equal of kings in running countries. Yet, throughout the nineteenth and most of the twentieth century, men ruled in the economic, business, legal and political arenas. Eighteenth- and nineteenth-century Mount Holly followed the national trend, which placed women in a role of dependency, with economic and legal subordination to men.

Of necessity, this did not apply to communities where every member was required for survival, as with the American pioneers in the West and those emigrants from England in Australia and elsewhere. The strong, reliable and capable pioneer woman remains an icon in American history, though an embarrassment among the well-heeled of the period.

By the 1850s Mount Holly had definitely become a town of merchants and well-to-do farmers. The entrance of the agricultural fair and the opera house indicate that life in town for many had become more than just work and sleep. Women of means were no longer involved in producing the everyday things needed by the family.

> *Ready made clothing, cheaper than ever at Pollock and Brother's, New Eagle Hall of Fashion, Main Street, Mount Holly and 34 Main Street, Burlington. Louis Pollock and Abraham Pollock thankful to their friends and patrons for past favors, hereby inform them and the public that they now have ready for inspection, a very large and beautiful assortment of fall and winter clothing.*[126]

In the postwar period of the 1870s, the town was well entrenched in the Victorian period, and leisure became an issue to be solved as opposed to being avoided.

In 1872 Victoria Woodhull, an Equal Rights Party candidate, ran for president against Ulysses S. Grant, even though at that time she, as with all other women, did not even have the right to vote. She stood no chance but made her point. Many women in Mount Holly and the immediate area likewise took on social and community leadership roles, but outside of the political scene and without public spectacle. It was an acceptable solution to filling leisure time.

Women found their control and outlet in an enveloping, informal leadership for social and cultural activity and education. In 1873 an innocuous request from several women in town led to a Freeholder ruling that dealt a blow to male-dominated cultural protocols: women could use the courthouse lawn to engage in the pursuit of croquet. Scandalous![127]

From reading the literature, the Mount Holly Women's League appears to have been more politically involved than most women's groups. Founded in 1903, the league established the role of public planning to address social and cultural needs in the town. We see the league pivotal in the establishment and support of a visiting nurse for those who are "shut in," and establishment of social supports for families during the Depression and during the two World Wars.

The first matron at the Burlington County Jail was brought into being, at least in part, as a result of direct (and probably clandestine as well) efforts of the league in 1906. Members joined with other women throughout the county who were appalled at reports, supposedly refuted, of indecent and immoral treatment of female inmates.[128] Though the majority of the supplicants were women from around the county, it was not until Reverend James Stoddard and Reverend Father Hart appealed for such a position that it was agreed to by the all-male Freeholder Board. Is it any wonder to modern husbands that their wives are experts at working behind the scenes?

The Burlington County Children's Home was in full swing as well. Founded in 1864 and hosted by one of the school buildings on Brainerd Street, the principle incorporators were women. In 1878 it moved to Garden and Clover Streets and in 1907, with the benefaction of Mary Dobbins's estate, to the present location on Pine Street:

> *The managers of the Union Association of the Children's Home, of Mount Holly, offer their Tenth Annual Report to their friends and contributors: Since the opening of*

Original Burlington County Children's Home on Garden Street. *Courtesy Cowgill Collection, Mount Holly Historical Society.*

Women gathered, learned and participated. Though shut out of men's groups, they formed their own. *Courtesy Mount Holly Historical Society.*

this institution in April, 1864, one hundred and thirty-one children have been admitted, ninety-seven boys and thirty-four girls, seventy-four provided with suitable homes, over whom supervision is still kept, thirty-five returned to their parents or friends, and three have died. Twelve children have been admitted during the past year, five have found homes and seven been taken by their parents. At present our family numbers twenty, all under eight years of age, the oldest of whom spend a portion of each day in school duties under the direction of a teacher residing in the institution.[129]

The Dobbins Memorial Home in Mount Holly, which will be the future home of the little inmates of the present Children's Home on Garden street [no street number stated], *will be formally dedicated and presented to the Children's Home Association on Tuesday next, May 29. The formal presentation of the property will be made by Judge Joseph H. Gaskill, as the representative of the Dobbins family, and Franklin B. Levis, as counsel for the Association, will receive the gift on behalf of the managers. The key of the institution will then be handed to Mrs. Morris H. Keeler, president of the Association.*[130]

Temperance (removal of all alcoholic beverage consumption) was an early issue for many of the women's groups, dating from before the Civil War. We see a similar thread in John Woolman's speeches to the tavern patrons in the 1760s. This would lead us to presume that there was a significant attendance by the male population at the various taverns and hotels dotting Mount Holly and other towns. This may also help to understand why social concerns were led early on by women, who were helping other women who were left to care for families while the breadwinner was on a drunk. Such roles were seen as natural extensions of the nurturing of a mother and, thus, were not a threat to men. This activity also served to reinforce the perception of women as more situated to the helping and nurturing work of the community than of practical or business endeavors. It had a secondary result, however, since the temperance societies eventually turned to women's suffrage as their issue.

The women of Mount Holly, assuming these "permitted" social and cultural roles, found ways to bring an impressive change to the community. It is this same energy and determination that made the women of Mount Holly leaders in their community up to and through the Second World War and to the present day.

STRONG OF BODY AND SPIRIT

From the earliest times of the settlement at Mount Holly one of the major causes of death had been disease. The newspapers were full of announcements, including this poignant notice apparently referring to the children of our esteemed historian, Zachariah Read: "Died in Mount Holly, on Friday August 13, 1847, George Shiras Read aged 20 months and on Monday August 23, 1847, Walter Read, on the 4th year of his age—only children of Dr. Read of Mount Holly."[131]

Despite the plethora of scare advertisements, debatable remedies and fashionable diagnoses in today's medical news, we often forget that life for most Americans in the twenty-first century is safer and less laden with death from disease than in prior generations. Of course, we have obesity and sloth to fault for many modern health problems, but these existed at that time as well, alongside more deadly diseases. One hundred years ago, the news was about ailments we rarely see today: cholera, typhus, whooping cough, measles, polio and typhoid.

> *There are four or five cases of typhoid fever in Mount Holly and one death from this dread disease has recently occurred in town. With so many cities infested with typhoid within a radius of twenty-five miles of Mount Holly it is not surprising that sporadic cases should make their appearance here. It is possible that all of the sufferers in this town contracted the disease elsewhere, but the number of cases now under treatment is sufficient to arouse some anxiety as to the cause and it certainly calls for the most searching inquiry by the local board of health which, we are informed, has already been commenced.*[132]

As we saw in the second chapter, medicinal practices early on were a mix of beliefs ancient and modern, natural and metaphysical. Allopathic medicine prevailed in official circles, but most people relied heavily on folk cures, herbal treatments and even homeopathic methods, which were practiced widely. For the less than wealthy, illness meant loss of pay and even destitution. Elixirs of wide variety (and diverse validity) were sold over the counter at the drugstores and shops in town. Local "healers" like Joseph White and "Doctor" James Still of Medford plied their trade throughout the area with great success and reputation.

The first homeopathic society in New Jersey was a branch of the American Institute of Homeopathy, which was organized at Mount Holly, July 20, 1846. Drs. Rhees and Ward were the only homeopathic practitioners in Mount Holly until 1860. Drs. E.K. Bancroft and Walter Ward were there from 1875 to 1880. In 1886 Drs. Samuel Caley and Willett W. Whitehead, and in 1899 Drs. John W. Branin, Samuel Carey, Oscar L. Grumbrecht, W.W. Whitehead and George U. Van Der Veer were in practice in Mount Holly.[133]

Medical services by this time had become "modern." The Burlington County Hospital, starting in 1881, provided the first local setting where treatment could be controlled. It had beds for seven patients and was located on Mount Holly Avenue, with Dr. Francis Ashurst, one of the founders, as the first superintendent.[134]

An interesting note in looking at the list of the first Board of Governors of the Burlington County Hospital is that they were all women. The wives of prominent local (and county) men served as the overall managers of the hospital. This is clearly in keeping with the Victorian view of women as the caretakers and nurturing souls of the community and family.

Nursing, having its formal American roots with Dorothy Dix and the Civil War period, was a staunchly feminine role. Midwifery is ancient, as is the "doula," the Greek word for the most important female slave or servant in an ancient Greek household; the woman who probably helped the lady of the house through her childbearing and rearing. So we might expect that one of the principal applications of the space in the hospital was for childbirth and thereafter.

Illustration of original Burlington County Hospital. The subsequent hospital, now Virtua Memorial Hospital is located on Madison Avenue and is known for a high quality of care. *Courtesy Mount Holly Library.*

> [The new mother] *remained in hospital for the "lying-in" period, which could range from 2 weeks to 2 months. A binder was placed around her waist "just snug enough to give her a sense of support" and napkins pinned to it to collect the postpartum discharge. Rest was considered essential, and* [as the pamphlets of the day read] *"for the first week most thoughtful and considerate friends will remain away from the sick room." It was expected that women in the postpartum period would have a nap every afternoon and at least six hours of sleep at night.*[135]

This was fine prescription for women who had additional supports from a husband, but not feasible for those who were the principal breadwinners for their families. The plight of poor women is not often discussed in histories; history tends to be written by those with the resources and the time to write, as can be seen with the Europeans and tales of their colonies. Mount Holly had very distinct class (and race) delineations that prevented many stories from being told.

References in both Shinn and Read to "Irish Town," "Sand Hill" and "Green Lane" sections of Mount Holly clearly interpret these as poor or working-class residential areas. The residences were mixed in among the employing factories in well-tested post-industrial alignment. From the earliest times of Mount Holly, we hear mostly of the well to do or prominent, excepting those ministers who choose poverty and are enshrined. Laborers, workers and unfortunate entrepreneurs (like Jacob Parker) who must live in huts or in squalor, are rarely mentioned. Yet we know they were here because the results of their efforts are evident.

One town chronicler, Howard G. Nixon, recounts a tale of his Uncle Ernest who was blinded in one eye from a backsplash of molten iron in the Johnson Iron Pipe foundry around 1900. With no workman's compensation laws or health benefits, the

Railroad Workers repairing crossing at Madison and Washington Streets. *Courtesy Mount Holly Library.*

man relied on family and associates (such as fellow lodge brothers) to support him through his recovery. Once recovered, he worked with his brother in the fruit business, with no pension or remuneration for his troubles.[136]

Activity and recreation included roller skating, and a roller hockey club existed in Mount Holly with a roller rink was located in the vicinity of the milldam. Sledding in the winter was best accomplished on Paxson Street hill or a trail on the mount. Winter activity included sleigh rides with horses and bells while wrapped in woolies and fur hats—practical as well as fun. Summer activity included swimming on small beaches at various points along the creek. Mill Dam Park was a favorite, and citizens could rent a canoe or rowboat to make the long summer day glide away.

Local artists flourished. Betsy Pease Gutmann was one, famous for her portrayal of infants, children and pets in various scenarios. She was well known by the 1920s in the magazine field throughout the United States. Though she traveled about the country, with studios in New York and Orange, New Jersey, she remained a native of Mount Holly through her family and that of her husband. The legacy of such artists lives on in the burgeoning art community of Mount Holly, which has built quite a following.[137]

Moving pictures came to town in 1904, with shows at the Opera House. Joseph Cowgill's wife, Irene, was noted to have played piano for the moving pictures shown there. Abe Saltzman's theater on Washington Street, opened in 1906, was the first place dedicated to motion pictures. And of course, for additional entertainment there was always the fair, the Thursday horse races with generous purses at the track and excursions to Philadelphia, New York and the Atlantic Ocean beaches. Quite a

Mine. Betsy Pease Gutman, Mount Holly native, contributed hundreds of works of children's art to publications such as *St. Nicholas Magazine*, *Pearson's Magazine* and others over the years. Her grasp of innocence and wonder accurately portray the view of children and children's roles at that time. *Author's collection.*

contrast to the early days, where socializing and business took place during the weekly and monthly meetings, and idle entertainment was a waste of valuable time. The increase in leisure time continued and so did opportunity to fill that leisure time.

9.

The Doughboys Arrive—And Stay

Austria declared war on Serbia and a chain reaction of alliances and pledges followed. Starting in part due to a long-standing family feud this was a war between closely related rulers of the various countries. By 1916 the Great War staggered on in a bloody stalemate.

Americans everywhere had been astounded, but there remained a consoling sense of distance. Since the end of the Indian Wars in 1890 and the quick victory over Spain in 1898–99, Americans had settled into a state of geopolitical inertia. Economics were good, jobs were plentiful (even for the influx of new immigrants) and life was generally tolerable for most.

Daily and weekly newspapers, including the *Mount Holly Herald* and the *New Jersey Mirror*, kept everyone abreast of the horrors and destruction. However, American neutrality could not stand against a world at war. Following a series of incidents, culminating in the sinking of the SS *Lusitania*, Congress and the president finally declared war. With entry into the European conflict the country's calm, self-satisfied existence was shattered—and Mount Holly would be forever changed.

There Goes the Neighborhood

At that point the U.S. Army realized it had only about 200,000 regular soldiers in uniform and not one organization of division size in place.[138] The national call to arms required a military buildup unseen since the Civil War, over fifty years earlier. By the end of the "Great War" it would have more than 5 million men under arms. One result of this buildup has had a lasting effect on Mount Holly and the towns around it: Camp Dix.

So what does the development of a military training and staging facility have to do with a history of Mount Holly? If you have to ask, you've never lived in proximity to a military base.

Division headquarters, Camp Dix under construction, 1917. *Courtesy Burlington County Library.*

> *It has been almost impossible to get woodchoppers in this section since Camp Dix opened. The men are getting such high wages at the Camp that they nearly all want to take the employment offered them there. It is said that about $10,000 has been brought here in wages from this source and the money has done a great deal of good in helping the men to take care of their families during the long hard winter.*[139]

When the army decided to set up a training facility in the pine barrens of New Jersey, they picked Wrightstown for its proximity to the east's great population centers and for its terrain, which could simulate the trenches of France. Camp Dix, named for a general in the Mexican and Civil Wars, was sited less than five miles from Mount Holly. In less than four months, the camp had to be turned from a sparsely settled tract of woodland and farms into a city of 1,600 buildings, housing 70,000 soldiers. One of the world's largest hospitals, with more than 2,000 beds, went up in a week. Rifle pits were dug and artillery ranges set up.[140]

H.G. Nixon recalled his father leaving the grocery and fruit business he ran to work at the construction of Camp Dix: "My grand father was a carpenter, and the boys had picked up some of his skills; I remember my father had a truck and transported the workmen back and forth to Camp Dix each day." Nixon lived on Shreve Street, which was still dirt in 1920. His father and Uncle Ernest opened a store at 95 Shreve Street for fruits and produce.[141]

Towns alongside the reservation supplied the housing and entertainment for the 11,000 workers and the materials for the construction. Mills generated lumber and cement. Farms provided food for the workers and animals for labor. Hordes of camp followers came through the area, including gamblers, prostitutes, and those plying illegal whisky for the recruits.[142] In an attempt to establish order and decorum, army brass proclaimed a prohibition of alcohol in a five-mile circle surrounding Dix, including Mount Holly.[143] Though Prohibition arrived as well only a couple of years later, there is no indication that Mount Holly obeyed the ordinance with any gusto.

Through the efforts of the different women's societies of New Jersey, soldiers' clubs were established on all sides of the camp—The Haversack and Woman's Suffrage clubs in Wrightstown, the Farmhouse Club and St. George's Club at Pointville. In addition social clubs at a little greater distance from Dix were established in Pemberton, Mount Holly and Trenton. The residents of Mount Holly began to offer formal and informal opportunities for the troops to relax, spend time writing home and join in local celebrations and events.

> *The formal opening of the Soldiers' club house in Mount Holly took place on Saturday afternoon and the exercises incident to that event were highly interesting...and a large crowd enjoyed the program which had been prepared. The band attached to the 311th Regiment at Camp Dix, consisting of 32 pieces, was in attendance and did much to enliven the occasion. The club house was unequal to the accommodation of more than a small portion of the crowd which would have liked to gain admittance to listen to the speaking and a much larger gathering filled the street outside. Chairman of the general committee Lorenzo L. Sapp presided and introduced the speakers in turn. To Rev. Luther M. Bicknell, pastor of the Presbyterian church, was assigned the presentation address, the speaker on behalf of the townspeople formally turning over the club house for the use of the soldiers. There was frequent music by the band and the soldiers' quartette and this portion of the program was by no means the least enjoyable of the afternoon's entertainment.*
>
> *Mrs. Gottlieb Everline is the matron of the club house and she seems to be the right person for this responsible post. She has a motherly interest in the boys and nothing seems to be too much trouble for her to do to add to the boys' comfort and happiness. The evening was a continuation of the afternoon's open-house. The band was still in attendance and gave an open air concert which was enjoyed by hundreds in the vicinity of Fountain Square.*[144]

The Women's League of Mount Holly, begun in 1903 as an outlet for community service by the town's ladies, worked to provide what was then referred to as "wholesome" entertainment for the workers and, later, for the recruits-in-training. Since members were from the various religious congregations in town, church organizations got involved as well.[145]

> *Rev. Thomas S. Hammond, Pastor. Parsonage, No. 17 Brainerd Street. All are welcome. Next Sunday Services: 10:30 AM Morning Worship. Service by an army minister from Camp Dix. 2 PM: Bible School, Mr. H.E. Alcott, Superintendent. 7:30 PM. Evening Worship. Sermon by Captain Jackson, army chaplain at Camp Dix. Prayer Meeting this evening at 7:30 in the church.*[146]

St. Andrew's Parrish sponsored the *St. George Club* at Camp Dix, and many families in town opened their homes, pantries and activity to young men from around the country.[147] However, the following entry gives one pause.

> *Miss Mary Gray, of the War Camp Community Service, who is to have charge of the personal work among the girls of the community adjacent to Camp Dix, has arrived. Miss Gray has had long experience in handling the problems of girl life, and she will be much appreciated here at the present time. Miss Gray will use Mount Holly as her working center, and will be glad to have the co-operation of all Mount Holly citizens.*[148]

Just what was the personal work of the girls? Most were probably serving in the canteens.

From the viewpoint of the boys in the division, the YMCA and Knights of Columbus regimental huts, located in different sections throughout the camp, provided by far the largest part of all the work done by welfare agencies. Here the men gathered for letter writing and reading as well as for nightly moving pictures and other forms of entertainment, with both local and professional talent.[149] Within a few months Camp Dix had developed into a self-sufficient community, effectively one of the ten largest cities in New Jersey.

Other locations were noted to have somewhat less-than-perfect reputations. The West End Hotel, on Washington Street, was noted for its bar and pool hall, and generally wild decorum.

The reports from Camp Dix were not always positive. The influx of this many people into what had been a rural community had an effect on the lives of the people in the town. In the following excerpt it is clear that the relative serenity and peace of the town, as county seat, was affected by the presence of the military. It is possible that this group of soldiers was on their way to the soldier's canteen in Mount Holly, or perhaps to the train station for leave.

> *An automobile driven by Robert P. Crane, while bringing seven soldiers from Camp Dix to Mount Holly Saturday afternoon skidded on the wet road near Chambers' Corner and overturned. It is reported that at the time the accident occurred the machine was going at the rate of sixty miles an hour. William M. Stout, of Illinois, a member of Company C, 345th Infantry, received injuries that resulted in his death. The others were John M. Sullivan, Ocella Price, Filmore R. Hulgrin, all of Company C, 345th Infantry; Peter G. Swedberg: Company C, 346th Infantry; Corporal Reuben Rickson, Headquarters Company, 336th Field Artillery, and Raymond J. Poler, Battery D, 336th Field Artillery, all of whom were more or less hurt, but their injuries not being of a serious nature.*[150]

The railroad was the principal route from Philadelphia and New York through to Camp Dix. Earlier, as we have seen, the Pennsylvania Rail Road created several lines in and around Mount Holly primarily as shipping and tourist travel conduits. The station at Mount Holly was noted to have seen as many as fifty to seventy trains a day in the high season and became a central dispatch point for arriving soldiers

An unidentified military unit debarks from the Camden and Mount Holly Line in town at the Madison Avenue station. The two homes seen are no longer there and immediately to the left of the scene would have been the Madison Hotel. Review by the Army Ordnance Museum, at Aberdeen, Maryland, establishes this as a World War One era artillery battery. *Courtesy Mount Holly Historical Society.*

and National Guard units from around the country.[151] Troops would disembark at the railhead on Madison Street and Washington from transports consisting mostly of refitted boxcars. They would then assemble and march the final five miles to Camp Dix.

PEACE AGAIN

Not all of activity in the area was related to war. In between wars Camp Dix served as a demobilization facility and was almost voted out of existence. They even had football clubs. In some cases they played at the public field in Mount Holly (where the county parking lot is today) and the game might have felt like the following description from an early report.

> *By 1919 the rivalry between Army and Navy was already a fixture in college football. On the afternoon of November 29, as the teams from Annapolis and West Point squared off in New York, the "Jackies" of the League Island Navy Yard took to the field against the "Doughboys" of Camp Dix, New Jersey. A soft drizzle did nothing to dampen the crowd's enthusiasm or detract from the afternoon's festivities. There were bands and bunting to mark the occasion and a hard fought game on the field.*[152]

Of course you have to wonder if there were a few ghosts of the Lenape cheering from the sidelines that day.

By 1919 the nation also had a new Eighteenth Constitutional Amendment prohibiting the sale or consumption of alcohol. However, Mount Holly in the Roaring Twenties enjoyed the same exuberance and panache as other small towns. Entertainment included movies, circuses and that new essential appliance radio. Though few were owned until later in the decade, the radio quickly became a fixture in almost every household. Papers recounted tales of bank robbers and "G-men," recorded music started to replace in-home entertainment, and movies started to speak.

The reduction of the available space through extensive housing construction following World War II further restricted the places one could roam as a child. Nevertheless, interest in traipsing along the creek, canoeing, boating, fishing and generally using the natural resources for recreation continued well into the mid-1970s when television and video games began to take over from the natural wonder of walking and running in the fields. More recently there has been a revival of activity along the creek, including discussion of re-opening the canoe rental business, and people are once again finding their time well spent downtown.

Dorothy McGrath recalled hanging around with her father at his cigar store at 86 High Street. She notes this was because there was a bakery at 82 High Street and a small toy store a few doors down and "Pop" would let her buy treats and small toys.[153] The downtown had a composition not unlike the modern shopping mall, with small specialty stores interspersed between larger, general stores and food markets. Acme, Inc., and A&P ran stores in town, but five or six of these would probably fit into the modern supermarket. Eggs, bread and milk were delivered.

H.G. Nixon recounts his role at the Jennings milk company on Mount Holly Avenue around 1924:

> *I would go out at 3:00 Am on weekends and meet Dick Jennings at Denny Mahoney's Diner, on White Street* [Mount Holly Diner]. *I would run the milk bottles to the customer's doorstep while Dick drove the truck. I received one dollar a day and, after the run ended about 7:00 AM, I would wash the old bottles out and fill them for the next delivery around 9:00 AM. We would cap each half-pint, pint or quart bottle with a paper cap with Jennings Dairy imprinted on it. There did not seem to be any sanitation laws.*[154]

Many families (if not most) still kept chickens and ducks—for eggs, for pets and for Sunday dinner. Some had pigs and cows as well, right in town. Kassie Regan recalls her mother canning the pork when her father had one of their pigs slaughtered.[155] There were several butchers in town, and you could arrange for them to dress your pig or cow, but there was no real in-home long-term refrigeration until the 1950s. This was the era when "the iceman cometh."

Hollyford Ice Company delivered door-to-door, at ten cents for a block of ice. On those hot, muggy New Jersey summer days, children ran behind the wagon begging for chips of ice. Hollyford quite possibly invented the "U-Store-It" concept; you could rent space in their large freezer to store your meats.[156] This increased the storage time for a cow or pig, and you didn't have to eat pickled pigs' feet all winter.

The agricultural fair continued as a draw for folks throughout the region well into the 1920s. At that point it even had an airfield and hot air balloons were added to the entertainment options. Every September the fair drew several thousands of people, and the horse racing season drew more throughout the year.

> *That was the place when I saw an airplane fly. The first place we had balloons. Hot air balloons.*
>
> *That's the first place we could get frozen dainties for five cents. They were just frozen ice. They were made in this little machine and they were frozen in blocks about that high and that think and they were wonderful. And they were only five cents.*[157]

The sense that Mount Holly was a thriving, bustling community up to and through the Great Depression is evident in the stories of these lifelong residents. It had a fireworks factory, which made its presence known upon its exit around 1922.

Dorothy McGrath remembers being shaken by the explosion of the fireworks factory: "An Italian family had a fireworks factory down on Water Street and it blew up and killed them all. The little girl was in my class. They lived in the house where they made the fireworks."[158]

Howard Nixon recalled the fireworks explosion as well:

> *One afternoon we were in class, there was a big explosion from the direction of Water Street, now Rancocas Road; the windows and buildings shook. It was learned that the fireworks plant had blown up, killing several people who lived there. This plant was located where the now Mount Holly Gardens is on Rancocas Road.*[159]

During the course of the 1920s, there were textile mills operating in town, owned in many instances by former employees and associates who learned their trade from Royle and Pilkington. In the spring of 1907, Mr. Royle came to Mount Holly, and with his partner, opened the Royle and Pilkington Mill and the Ankokas Dye Mill, which in subsequent years gave employment to hundreds, including Carl Heyer. This was the first full-scale textile mill in Mount Holly.[160] The textile mills survived the Depression, providing work for many locals, through the determination of their employees and managers.

A legacy of Mr. Royle was the R&P Baseball Club—unrivaled in the region. Mount Holly hosted regional playoffs at Royle and Pinkerton Field, which was located where the county parking lot is today. The Mount Holly semi-pro team (descendant of the team J.C. Cowgill played on in 1866) was a member of the South Jersey League and games with Burlington and Florence and others were hotly contested.[161]

This park boasted permanent grandstands and a field so well laid out that minor league teams and teams from the old Negro league would often play there.

In December 1865, the Philadelphia Athletics (distant precursors to the Phillies) scheduled a double-header of winter ball against Burlington and Mount Holly teams. Burlington went off smoothly, but the Mount Holly game had to be stopped in the seventh inning because of a snowstorm. Undaunted, both teams simply went to the Mount Holly Hotel for a fine banquet instead (probably oyster stew).[162]

Bob Gaskill recalled going to R&P Field as a child to watch the games and how, to a young boy, the atmosphere was almost like being in Yankee Stadium.[163] H.G. Nixon recalled some team members and noted that Mount Holly had the best pitcher in the area.[164] R&P Field also hosted football matches between high school teams and even regional football clubs (much like today's softball leagues), and served as the track for the high school prior to construction of the RVRHS facility in 1936.

In the reorganization of Mount Holly that occurred with the construction of the current county complex in the 1960s, the field was torn down. Little league fields were constructed near the creek at Monroe Park, replacing the ancient wharf buildings that were there, but these are not unique. Most old-timers seem to feel the loss of R&P Field (and the fairgrounds) threw a wet blanket on Mount Holly. Certainly, economic stress would increase ten-fold very soon.

OCTOBER 1929

From 1921 to 1929, the Dow Jones rocketed from 60 to 400! Millionaires were created instantly. Soon stock market trading became America's favorite pastime as investors jockeyed to make a quick killing. Investors mortgaged their homes, and foolishly invested their life savings in hot stocks.

The stock market crash of 1929 launched the Great Depression. The Depression was the time from October 1929 to the mid-1930s. Mass poverty occurred then, as many workers lost their jobs and were forced to live in shanty towns. Former millionaire businessmen were reduced to selling apples and pencils on street corners. One third of Americans were below the poverty line in the Great Depression. The Dow Jones finally surpassed its 1929 high, a full 26 years later in 1955.[165]

So, what does one do when there are so many workers and no jobs? Mount Holly industry suffered along with the rest of the country. Factory closings and shutdowns were common. General maintenance of buildings and homes deteriorated and foreclosures skyrocketed.

The Civilian Conservation Corps (CCC) was organized by the administration of Franklin D. Roosevelt as a means of employing (and occupying) the hundreds of thousands of men who were unemployed as a result of the Great Depression. Since the demobilization of Camp Dix following the Great War, it became a logical location for the CCC in the Philadelphia and New York area. The public works included reclaiming the local waterways and resources. State parks (such as Lebanon State Forest) were carved from the pinelands, and the Mount was cleared, cleaned and planted with nice shrubbery.[166]

Aerial view of Mount Holly, circa 1930. R&P Field is visible in the center, as is the line where the creek bends back on itself, which was called Gaskill's Neck. Several flood control channels were prepared by the Army Corps of Engineers to reduce flooding in the town and so the creek appears more extensive than it was originally. *Courtesy Mount Holly Library.*

This decade also saw the end of a generation, much as we are now experiencing it. Old veterans, those who had gone to war for Abe Lincoln and the Union, were almost gone. The history of these soldiers has been told a hundred times, but the impact they had on local communities is not often understood. Today we know the opportunity for hearing from the generation of veterans of World War II is fading. So, too, the same vanishing opportunity was felt by that generation about another.

> *Thomas H. Phares, 91, one of the few surviving Civil War veterans, died at his home, 20 Brainerd street, Mount Holly, on Saturday, from a heart attack. Soon after the outbreak of the Civil War Mr. Phares enlisted in the 23d New Jersey Volunteers, and later with the Second New Jersey Cavalry. His war service covered over four years. Although he took part in a number of engagements, he never was wounded. Mr. Phares was prominent at Memorial Day exercises in Mount Holly, riding at the head of the parade and then taking part in the program by leading in prayer.*[167]

Memorial Day Parade preparations, circa 1950. *Courtesy Mount Holly Historical Society.*

GIs

Camp Dix expanded exponentially during the buildup and training for World War II as early as September 1939. It was now Fort Dix, and included an Army Air Corps base, which eventually became McGuire Air Force Base. It was (and is) the largest combined military facility on the East Coast.

The sheer volume of traffic in and out of Dix during the war would require another book-length discussion. Suffice it to say that there are many remaining veterans of World War II and Korea who recall at least a few weeks at Fort Dix.

Additional land was acquired from local farmers and additional construction provided by area companies. Troop trains arrived daily, passing through Mount Holly to the Pemberton station. Eventually a line was built through to what was now Fort Dix from Trenton and New York. Life in Mount Holly was much the same as it had been during the First World War. Soldiers came through on leave and local girls served as waitresses and hostesses at the United Services Organization (USO) and other facilities similar to what had been opened in 1917.

Of course, in the history of the war there has been little about the estimated 15,000 POWs held at Dix from early 1944 to the end of the war. Many were employed at farm and factory work here in Burlington County. Most were German, some were Italian and a few were even Russian.[168] Older residents probably recall a few of those POWs on work details.

Downtown during the 1940s. One advantage of small town living was the ration card for gas went further. *Courtesy Mount Holly Historical Society.*

The local telephone service suffered. It was reported by district office manager Paul Coffee that more than 9,000 calls were typical in a business day. (Compare this to the original twenty-five phones in 1883.) Of these, 1,200 were toll calls emanating from Fort Dix phones.[169]

The impact on the area would last well into the present. Many homeowners in Mount Holly who have an apartment or extra studio rent to the military personnel of Dix or McGuire. Personnel from both facilities regularly shop in, visit and travel through town. Dependents often obtain work in local businesses while their family is stationed here, and children attend local schools. All-in-all, it's been a respectable addition to the neighborhood.

POSTWAR: THE SUBURBS ARRIVE

The land around Mount Holly, as we have seen contained large tracts of farmland, cranberry bogs, blueberry fields and woodlands. Expansion into these undeveloped places opened up the suburbs. Often, we think of the drain of vital family and economic activity from large cities such as New York or Philadelphia. Small towns reeled from the loss as well.

Mount Holly remained the county seat after World War II but things were changing throughout America. Small towns no longer had the charm and attraction

Mill Street, 1958. *Courtesy Mount Holly Library.*

Rancocas Valley Regional High School, 1960s. *Courtesy Mount Holly Historical Society.*

Burlington County Hospital, 1960s. *Courtesy Burlington County Library.*

for the many men and women who had seen the world. Many places simply did not possess the free land to accommodate the construction of homes for the millions of new families being started and extended. Farms and estates were becoming harder to maintain and became the new promised land for housing developers.

A large portion of the local industry fell into slow times following the war. Manufacturing of textiles and lumber moved into the South, where cheap labor brought the cost of production down. Millwork continued, as did foundry work. And a new avenue arrived, bringing people from all over into the area seeking new homes and new lives. The New Jersey Turnpike opened in 1951, with an exit two miles from downtown.

The turnpike, the first limited access road of its kind in America, meant people could travel quickly and efficiently from Philadelphia to New York, and places in between. The time from Mount Holly to Philadelphia was cut once again, as it had been with steamboats, then the railroad. Now the automobile became the vehicle of choice for most Americans, and this expansion of mobility meant radical change in how things were done.

It also meant that people were no longer restricted to rail lines, trolley lines, or their hometown shops and restaurants. They could move—and they did. The influx of new homes following the war was the greatest, as a percentage of land acquired, since the immigrants first arrived in 1677.

Andrew Levitt constructed a planned community in Willingboro Township. The Ashurst descendants sold off the gardens of Clover Hill in 1948, where a large expanse of new homes was subsequently constructed. The Levis estate was liquidated, resulting in the construction of the Mount Holly Gardens following the war. The fairgrounds became a shopping mall and a cluster of homes.

Schools became desegregated during the 1950s, at least in New Jersey. Mount Holly's regional high school absorbed students from the area, as it does now. Additional elementary schools were built to accommodate the growth in population as the "Baby Boomers" entered the census. The old grammar school at Brainerd and Buttonwood was abandoned and the property sold, making room for the Woolman Commons community. There was a concurrent growth in parochial and Friends school attendance, including more enrollment at Sacred Heart School.

10.

Decline and Rebirth

The agricultural and industrial base for Mount Holly gave way to the commuter economy in much the same way as it did for other, larger communities. The town succumbed to expansive and expensive, homes and communities, which emerged along with a new wave of immigrants; those from New York and Philadelphia, and North Jersey. This in-migration of money and social transience was no less devastating than those forbearers, three hundred years earlier, had been to the Lenape.

Mount Holly remained significant for the role it played as county seat. Buildings along High Street, across from the old 1796 courthouse, reflect that role in the almost endless rows of legal shingles and title offices. Where residents recalled wandering downtown in their youth to visit the soda shop or the ice cream store, they now encountered primarily bondsmen (and women) and, increasingly, vacant storefronts.

Mount Holly had traffic, but no customers; homes, but fewer owners; residents, but fewer community members. Jobs and careers pushed people to move in and out of towns with the ebb and flow of the money. Extended families were further extended by hundreds or thousands of miles, as sons and daughters picked up and chose lives in other states. The family farm just didn't have the pull anymore. And the deathblow seemed to coincide with urban unrest in the late 1960s and early '70s.

Camden, once the flower of South Jersey, and home to numerous industries such as Campbell's Soup and RCA-Victor, began the slide into the unfilled grave in which it now rests. Newark died an ugly, burned-out death, only very recently rising from the ashes. Almost in sympathy, Mount Holly went into hibernation. Magnificent homes, once ringing with family and friends and hired help, turned into multifamily apartments, managed on behalf of absent landlords. Gardens were sold off by relatives who had no use for the inheritance. Businesses closed, or turned to serve those most common customers in a courthouse town—lawyers and defendants. Those businesses that survived did so by sheer willpower.

Migrant workers serving the cranberry and truck farms nearby found refuge in the affordable apartments remaining from the postwar years and those carved from many a Victorian edifice. Immigrants from dozens of countries arrived, each with

Downtown, 1960s. Note the New York Store, mentioned by many as the place to get up-to-date fashion in town. It would have been similar to a high-end women's chain store today. Dorothy McGrath recalls her mother visiting the store, then making a pattern of what she saw and sewing her own dress to be "in fashion" at an affordable price. *Courtesy Mount Holly Historical Society.*

his or her own culture and concept of America. With a large stock of pre-twentieth-century homes, the town became a readymade setting for temporary and transient housing. It was not so much different from many of its neighboring boroughs. Locals simply moved to the newer homes in the cul-de-sacs that were carved from fallow farmland. And yet, this very action is why so many historic structures remain; there was no incentive to demolish them.

IT'S THE PIGS

Uptown, elegance, limos and pearls may be the buzzwords. Downtown, the word is revitalization. Mount Holly is no exception. Traveling through Mount Holly (either on Route 541 or Route 537) people stop and see the change. They remark on this marquee or that new store, almost as though arriving for the first time. Increased merchant activity—shops offering unique items at a great value—has returned. Not all manage to survive. The principles of entrepreneurship remain as they always have been. Nevertheless, there are an increasing number of businesses that see the small-town setting as the place to display and market their unique wares; a place that distinguishes them from the cookie-cutter mall shops.

Today's Mount Holly is like a debutante, dancing on the edge of maturity. Resurgence of interest in the downtown and community has been brought home by the Main Street Mount Holly program, and efforts of the Urban Enterprise

Mill Street looking toward High and Washington, 1990s. The arcade had burned in a large fire that consumed much of the west side of High Street. In a typical boxy minimalist design of the 1960s, the current strip mall, which includes LaVitas Restaurant, replaced it. Revision, rebirth and change continue to be a part of the life cycle of the town. *Courtesy Mount Holly Historical Society.*

Zone Board, the Mount Holly Township Council and the many volunteers and professionals that make the special events and daily development happen. Businesses, like Alaimo Engineering, have played a role in conserving many of the stately mansions at the upper end of High Street and homes along Mill Street. Visitors can envision the lifestyles and circumstances of the families there instead of seeing them demolished to make way for modern construction. For all of these players, the focus is on building a community of shops and residences working together to evoke the sense of village.

Combining shopping, a meal and fun activity are what the concept of "village" is all about. It is what sustained the various malls that rose from cow pastures in the sixties and seventies to fill this void within the sprawling suburban developments. It is what will bring the shopping public back into the small town, and along with them the residents and families that have been the backbone of the place.

This tends to create a bustling, lively atmosphere conducive to drawing public foot traffic into a downtown area. Of course, foot traffic leads to increased sales, but also to an increased sense of safety and security. Both lead to more people spending more time downtown among friends and neighbors, enjoying an assortment of activity.

In 2003 drivers coming into Mount Holly on High Street were entranced by a sculpture of a giant prehistoric rat. Grabbing the public's attention with sculpture was the brainchild of Rocky D'Entrement, local photographer, entrepreneur and community organizer. Lynne Lemyre, a renowned artist who owns Home Fine Art Gallery along with her husband Jim, and at the time director of Main Street Mount Holly program, brought in the idea of the "Year of the Cow" sculptures as seen in other cities. Regan Young, architect and leader in the Main Street Mount Holly program, arrived at the idea of linking this to the lunar calendar. The Township Council agreed. In the tradition of Mount Holly past, the associations and links formed by these folks opened the town to residents of the county.

Monkey sculptures pose for pictures prior to their auction, 2004. *Courtesy R.F. D'Entrement.*

That brings us to the pigs.

In colonial times it was common to have pigs rooting through the streets of any community—they were the garbage collectors. The Friends Meeting on Garden Street did employ a flock of sheep as their landscape crew for some time. There have been many witnesses to wild turkey (the animals not the beverage), a flock of which has apparently set up territorial claim to part of the Mount. Based on evidence of tree felling, beavers are back in the mill races and waterways in town. An unexplained rooster could be overheard calling out the sun at the ungodly hour of 4:00 a.m. a year or so ago. But pigs? They have not been seen in Mount Holly for at least the past few decades.

In 2004 the three-dimensional works of art evolved into primates that signified the Chinese year of the monkey. Regional artists painted and embellished the fiberglass monkeys for display until sold at auction to raise funds for the revitalization effort. The Monkeys evolved into Dogs which evolved into Roosters which evolved into Pigs, following the traditional Chinese calendar.

It's all part of Mount Holly's annual First Night Burlington County, an arts-based community New Year's Eve Festival, including parades, concerts and fireworks. First Night is now one of the best attended events in the county. Sound like the days of old? Think we might resurrect Kleingunther's New Year Association?

Families would walk from Pine Street or Hulme or Mount Holly Avenue or Monroe, to see the vendors and shop the shops. Kids would have a "dainty," an ice cream soda, or a "pop," and watch the New Year arrive. Families would arrive by

Fire (chili contest) and Ice (carving competition) Festival, 2007. *Photograph by author.*

steam engine from around the country to spend the holidays in town. Today they arrive by automobile and bus, but who knows, maybe the train will re-emerge.

IT'S THE PEOPLE

Many, many local folks have worked diligently and relentlessly in formulating a venue for public gatherings. Main Street Mount Holly, Mount Holly Township and the County of Burlington have sponsored numerous events in partnership with several local associations (there's that word again). The Mount Holly Historical Society, the Burlington County Master Gardeners, the Mill Race Village Merchants, the Mount Holly Library and Lyceum, the Greater Mount Holly Downtown Business and Professional Association, the Lions, Elks and Rotary, the County Parks and Recreation Department and countless volunteers, specialists and business people develop a collective energy that is hard to resist.

A significant element in the reinvention of Mount Holly has been creating a welcoming atmosphere. The defeatist attitude fostered by ongoing war with the suburbs and the malls has been replaced by a solid belief that small towns offer more. Families and individuals from all over are invited by the town to discover the

The growth of the area is bringing larger crowds into town and making the streets full again. You just can't get this at the Cherry Hill Mall. Mount Holly Car Show and Street Fair, 2006. *Courtesy R.F. D'Entrement.*

New Historic Mount Holly by participating in activities such as the annual Fire and Ice Festival—Mount Holly's Chili Contest and the Annual Ice Carving street fair in January. The most recent chili contest brought more than one hundred entries from the region, and was held in the building of the Relief Fire Company—255 years after it was founded. Now, that's tradition.

Each May, car enthusiasts from all over come to Mount Holly to see the eclectic mix of antique cars. The Historical Society opens several decorated homes and locations for tours each December. Whenever Friday the Thirteenth falls, count on Mount Holly to host its ghost tour. (Ghosts never vacation.) A reenactment of the Battle of Mount Holly has occurred for the past four Decembers; by the way, Colonel Griffin has been successful each year so the colonials plan to return. The Mount Holly Bicycle Race commemorates H.B. Smith and his Star racing bicycle each July. Witches and fairies in the streets at Halloween recall the costume parades of Dorothy McGrath, and arts and crafts sit side-by-side with local concerts of regional and national musical artists such as Patrick Fitzsimmons, Lili Anel, Guy Davis, Nora Wittacker and Garnett Rogers. Who knows? Hacks Canoe Rentals may reopen soon and you can paddle the milldam pond to your heart's content.[170]

All of this activity builds on the confidence espoused in the Main Street effort and rebirth of young families and renovated homes. Current ordinance prohibits any building in the historic district that is restored to single family status from ever

First Night Burlington County, welcoming in 2007. Mount Holly is once again the seat of activity and entertainment for the region. *Courtesy R.F. D'Entrement.*

being approved for multifamily. Mount Holly was once the center of activity in this region, along with Burlington City. Although there will always be growth, sprawl and commercial development in New Jersey, the residents of Mount Holly are dedicated to making their town the hospitable centerpiece for those living around them.

You may live in Westampton (no "h," remember), Eastampton, Southampton or any other 'ampton. You might have moved here from any one of a hundred urban, suburban or rural communities across the United States or Canada; or Mexico, Germany, Ecuador, China, Ukraine or Italy. You might have grown up in the old Timbuctoo properties. You may have been in Willingboro since the end of World War II and raised a family there. You could be living in Pemberton, or in one of the new developments in Lumberton, Mount Laurel, Springfield or Mansfield. No matter—Mount Holly represents the hub of activity and traffic and serves as the greatest resource for community-based activity in the area; and a great opportunity to become involved in deciding the future of the region.

Simply put—it's neighborly.

Notes

Chapter 1

1. Rementer, "Pahsahn: The Lenape Indian Football Game."
2. Page, *In the Hands of the Great Spirit*, 121.
3. Walker, *Proceedings of the NJ Historical Society*, 193.
4. Crazy Horse, *Powhatan Renape Confederation Home Page.*
5. Cresson, *In Their Footsteps.*
6. Ibid.
7. Woodward and Hageman, *History of Burlington & Mercer Counties.*
8. Walker, 193.
9. Woodward and Hageman.
10. "Humor and the Delaware Tribe."
11. Crazy Horse.

Chapter 2

12. Read, "History of Mount Holly."
13. Walker, 193.
14. Shinn, *History of Mount Holly*, 5.
15. Birch and Stevens, *The Reeves Family.*
16. Read, "History of Mount Holly."
17. Woodward and Hageman, *History of Burlington & Mercer Counties.*
18. Read, "History of Mount Holly."
19. Birch and Stevens, *The Reeves Family.*
20. Shinn, *History of Mount Holly*, 5.
21. Woodward and Hageman, *History of Burlington & Mercer Counties.*
22. Shinn, *History of Mount Holly*, 5.
23. Lane, *From Indian Trail to Iron Horse*, 15.
24. Cowgill, J., noted in Shinn, IBID.
25. Stryker-Rodda, *Revolutionary Census of New Jersey.*
26. Commentary entry in the *New Jersey Mirror*, 1887.
27. Perinchief, *The Woolman Family.*
28. Read, "History of Mount Holly."

29. Smith, M., "Compilation of Mount Holly Taverns, Inns, Hotels, and Package Stores," manuscript, Mount Holly Historical Society, 2000.
30. *Pennsylvania Journal and Advertiser*, January 11, 1743, in Boyer, *Early Forges and Furnaces in New Jersey*.
31. Ibid.
32. Perinchief, *A History of St. Andrew's Church.*
33. Read, "History of Mount Holly."
34. Weiss and Weiss, *Forgotten Mills of New Jersey*, 47.

Chapter 3
35. Eliot, ed., *Autobiography of Benjamin Franklin, The Journal of John Woolman.*
36. De Cou, *Historical Sketches of Mount Holly and Vicinity.*
37. Eliot, ed., *Autobiography of Benjamin Franklin, The Journal of John Woolman.*
38. Ibid.
39. Wright, *Afro-Americans in New Jersey*.
40. Ibid.
41. Wright and Wonkeryor, *Steal Away, Steal Away*.
42. Brainerd, *John Brainerd's Journal*, 10.
43. Ibid., 11.
44. Shinn, *History of Mount Holly*.
45. Ibid.
46. Perinchief, *A History of St. Andrew's Church.*
47. Shinn, *History of Mount Holly*.
48. Eliot, ed., *Autobiography of Benjamin Franklin, The Journal of John Woolman.*
49. Ibid.
50. Ibid.
51. Ibid.
52. Read, "History of Mount Holly."
53. Eliot, ed., *Autobiography of Benjamin Franklin, The Journal of John Woolman.*
54. Smith, *Mount Holly Women Who Cared.*
55. Parry, *Betsey Ross: Quaker Rebel.*

Chapter 4
56. Shinn, *History of Mount Holly*, 40.
57. Ibid.
58. Joseph C. Cowgill Scrap Book, Mount Holly Historical Society Collection. Joseph Cowgill was a collector of memorabilia. His scrap book provides a vast array of detailed information about the town during his lifetime and before, and diverse information, both funny and sad. Much of what we know about Mount Holly from 1840 to 1900 is located somewhere in his scrapbook.
59. Shinn, *History of Mount Holly*.
60. Ibid.
61. *New Jersey Mirror*, March 31, 1819.

62. Still, *Early Recollections and Life of Dr. James Still.*
63. Mount Holly Library and Lyceum pamphlet; Shinn, *The History of Mount Holly.*
64. Lane, *From Indian Trail to Iron Horse*, 91.
65. Newspaper Extracts, 1775, Archives of the State of New Jersey, First Series, Vol. 31, 1–47.
66. Bolger, *Smithville.*

Chapter 5

67. Ewald, *Diary of the American War.*
68. "The Recruiting of the British Army in the American Revolution." http://www.americanrevolution.org
69. "The Romance of Old Philadelphia," chapter 13, http://kellscraft.com/OldPhiladelphia/OldPhiladelphiaCh13.html
70. Shinn, *History of Mount Holly.*
71. Jackson, *Margaret Morris.*
72. Letter from Von Donop to General Howe in New York, December 1776, Stryker Revolutionary War Manuscript Collection.
73. Washington, George, correspondence by Joseph Reed and Israel Putnam, George Washington Papers.
74. Fischer, *Washington's Crossing.*
75. Ibid.
76. Tustin, *Widow of Mount Holly.*
77. *New Jersey Mirror*, May 19, 1819.
78. *New Jersey Mirror* archives, 1865, Burlington County Library System.

Chapter 6

79. *New Jersey Mirror*, Cowgill collection, Mount Holly Historical Society.
80. Shinn, *History of Mount Holly.*
81. *The Journal of J. Warner Erwin*, http://www.brynmawr.edu/iconog/frdr.html#full.
82. *New Jersey Mirror*, March 24, 1819.
83. *The Journal of J. Warner Erwin*, http://www.brynmawr.edu/iconog/frdr.html#full.
84. *New Jersey Mirror*, August 16, 1820.
85. Ibid., August 9, 1820.
86. Ibid., March 21, 1821.
87. Lane, *From Indian Trail to Iron Horse*, 211.
88. *New Jersey Mirror*, February 25, 1847.
89. Ibid., March 1, 1855.
90. Ibid., June 15, 1881.
91. Shinn, *History of Mount Holly.*
92. Ibid.
93. *Burlington City, N.J.*, http://08016.com/railroads.html.
94. Kozempel, "The Camden and Burlington County Railway Company"; Shinn, *History of Mount Holly.*
95. *Burlington City, N.J.*, http://08016.com/railroads.html.

96. *New Jersey Mirror*, November 25, 1818.
97. Ibid., March 31, 1819.
98. Ibid., April 1865.
99. Shinn, *History of Mount Holly*.
100. Smith, " Facts Written by Mary Smith."

Chapter 7
101. Eliot, C.W., ed. *The Journal of John Woolman*.
102. Wright and Wonkeryor, *Steal Away, Steal Away*.
103. *New Jersey Mirror*, February 27, 1851.
104. Article in J.C. Cowgill Collection, Mount Holly Historical Society, 1847.
105. Wright and Wonkeryor, *Steal Away, Steal Away*.
106. *New Jersey Mirror*, November 21, 1850.
107. Shinn, *History of Mount Holly*.
108. *New Jersey Mirror*, February 13, 1862
109. Wright, *Afro-Americans in New Jersey*.
110. "About Us," *African Methodist Episcopal Church*, http:// www.ame-church.com/about-us.
111. Wright, *Afro-Americans in New Jersey*.
112. *New Jersey Mirror*, October 31, 1861.
113. Ibid., August 7, 1862. The prisoners were "exchanged" and returned home a few months later. As a result they were spared the fate of many of their fellows in being moved from Libby Prison to the notorious prison camp at Andersonville, Georgia.
114. *New Jersey Mirror*, June 23, 1864
115. Cowgill collection clippings, Mount Holly Historical Society.

Chapter 8
116. The author corresponded with an historian in Mount Holly, North Carolina, who noted the name of that town came from Mount Holly, NJ because of the amount and quality of the Semple thread used in the fabric and cloth mills there.
117. Shinn, *History of Mount Holly*.
118. *New Jersey Mirror*, January 4, 1893.
119. Historical Notes, *New Jersey Mirror*, June 30, 1937.
120. Bolger, *Smithville*.
121. McShulkis, *Mount Holly Gardens*.
122. McShulkis, *Monograph for Mount Holly Master Gardeners*.
123. Ibid.
124. Cowgill collection clippings, Mount Holly Historical Society.
125. Stryker-Rodda, *Revolutionary Census of New Jersey*.
126. *New Jersey Mirror*, January 4, 1855.
127. Smith, *Mount Holly Women Who Cared*.
128. Ibid.
129. *New Jersey Mirror*, January 15, 1874.
130. Ibid., May 23, 1906.

131. Ibid., September 9, 1847.
132. Ibid., March 18, 1908.
133. King, "History of Homeopathy and its Institutions in America," http://www.homeoint.org/history/king/4-12.htm
134. Shinn, *History of Mount Holly.*
135. Nusche, *Lying In.*
136. Nixon, *The Life and Times of Howard Gaskill Nixon in and around Mount Holly, New Jersey.*
137. Smith, *Mount Holly Women Who Cared.*

Chapter 9
138. USACTI, *The History of Fort Dix, New Jersey, 1917–1967.*
139. *New Jersey Mirror*, March 6, 1918.
140. Blackwell, *1917: The Doughboys of Dix.*
141. Nixon, *The Life and Times of Howard Gaskill Nixon in and around Mount Holly, New Jersey.*
142. USACTI, *The History of Fort Dix, New Jersey, 1917–1967.*
143. Blackwell, *1917: The Doughboys of Dix.*
144. *New Jersey Mirror*, March 6, 1918.
145. Smith, *Mount Holly Women Who Cared.*
146. *New Jersey Mirror*, March 6, 1918.
147. Perinchief, *A History of St. Andrew's Church.*
148. *New Jersey Mirror*, July 18, 1918.
149. Sullivan, ed., *The History of New York State*, 1368.
150. *New Jersey Mirror*, July 17, 1918.
151. Shinn, *History of Mount Holly.*
152. Fenton, *Ships and Yards*, http://ghosts.footballhistory.org/Maritime.htm
153. Winzinger, interview with Dorothy McGrath, Mount Holly Historical Society Archives.
154. Nixon, *The Life and Times of Howard Gaskill Nixon.*
155. Winzinger, interview with John and Kassie Regan, Mount Holly Historical Society Archives, 1998.
156. Ibid.
157. Winzinger, interview with Brook Tidswell and Carl Heyer, Mount Holly Historical Society Archives, 1998.
158. Winzinger, interview with Dorothy McGrath, Mount Holly Historical Society Archives, 1998.
159. Nixon, *The Life and Times of Howard Gaskill Nixon.*
160. *New Jersey Mirror*, May 18, 1939.
161. DiClerico and Pavelec, *The Jersey Game.*
162. Ibid.
163. Robert Gaskill, interview with author, March 2007.
164. Nixon, *The Life and Times of Howard Gaskill Nixon.*
165. Stock Market Crash Net.
166. Shinn, *History of Mount Holly.*
167. *New Jersey Mirror*, December 30, 1936.

168. USACTI, *The History of Fort Dix, New Jersey, 1917–1967.*
169. Ibid.

Chapter 10
170. Main Street Mount Holly site, http://www.mainstreetmountholly.com/index.php, 2007.

Bibliography

Birch, Clara B., and Clara Swain Stevens. *The Reeves Family: Walter Reeve of Burlington County, New Jersey and a Number of His Descendants Through Ten Generations, from notes left by Samuel V. Reeves*. Merchantville, NJ: H. Stanley Craig, Printer, 1930.

Blackwell, Jon. "1917: The Doughboys of Dix." *The Trentonian*. http://capitalcentury.com/1917.html

Bolger, W.C. *Smithville: The Result of Enterprise*. Burlington County Cultural and Heritage Commission, 1980.

Boyer, Charles Shimer. *Early Forges & Furnaces in New Jersey*. 1931. Reprint, Philadelphia: University of Pennsylvania Press, 1961.

Brainerd, John. *John Brainerd's Journal*. Works Progress Administration, Historical Records Survey, 1941.

Burlington City, NJ History, 2007. http://08016.com/railroads.html.

Burlington County Library. Endowed postcard, photographic and family genealogy collections. Westampton, NJ.

Burlington County Library. Vertical File on Mount Holly. Westampton, NJ.

Chief Roy Crazy Horse. *Powhatan Renape Confederation*. http://www.powhatan.org/history.html.

Clark, Hazel C. *Mount Holly: A Picture Story of its Historical Growth*. New Jersey: Mount Holly Historical Society, 1975.

Cowgill, Joseph C. Personal Scrap Book. In the Mount Holly Historical Society Collection.

Cresson, Os. *In Their Footsteps, A brief history of the lives of people who lived on the property called Lumberton Leas*, 2005. http://www.mlra.org/footsteps/index.htm#one

De Cou, George. *Historical Sketches of Mount Holly and Vicinity*. Mount Holly: G. De Cou, 1936.

Delaware Tribe of Indians. http://www.delawaretribeofindians.nsn.us/

DiClerico, J.M., and B.J. Pavelec. *The Jersey Game*. New Brunswick, NJ: Rutgers University Press, 1991.

Dobbins, Edward T. *Mary A. Dobbins Memorial House*. Mount Holly: The New Jersey Mirror Print, 1906.

Eliot, C.W., ed. *The Autobiography of Benjamin Franklin; The Journal of John Woolman; Fruits of solitude by William Penn.* With introductions and notes, Harvard Classics, Vol. 1. New York: P.F. Collier, 1909.

Erwin, J. Warner. *The Journal of J. Warner Erwin, 1839–1854*, 2007. http://www.brynmawr.edu/iconog/frdr.html#full

Ewald, Johann. *Diary of the American War: A Hessian Journal.* Edited and translated by Joseph P. Tustin. New Haven: Yale University Press, 1979.

Faris, John T. *The Romance of Old Philadelphia.* http://www.kellscraft.com/OldPhiladelphia/OldPhiladelphiaCh13.html.

Farmers' Trust Company, Mount Holly, N.J. *100th anniversary of the Farmers' Trust Company, Mount Holly, New Jersey, 1814–1914.* Mount Holly, 1915.

Fenton, John J. *Ships and Yards: Football Along the Delaware*, 2007. http://ghosts.footballhistory.org/Maritime.htm, 2007.

Fischer, D.H. *Washington's Crossing.* New York: Oxford University Press, 2004.

Gaskill, Nelson Burr. *Imprints from the press of Stephen C. Ustick, with its several locations: together with some items which were published, but not printed by him, 1794-1836, to which are added interesting notes & comments.* 1875. Reprint, Washington, D.C.: [s.n.], 1940.

Gesensway, Eleanor. *Life along the North Branch of the Rancocas Creek between Mount Holly and Smithville, New Jersey, Burlington County Library System.* Mount Holly: Eleanor Gesensway, 1992.

Gummere, Amelia Mott. *The John Woolman Memorial.* Mount Holly, NJ: John Woolman Memorial Association, 1928.

Harrington, M.R. *The Indians of New Jersey: Dickon Among the Lenape.* New Brunswick: Rutgers University Press, 1986.

Helfand, Esther. *A Survey of the Mount Holly Library.* Trenton: New Jersey State Library, Library Development Bureau, 1973.

Hiltzhimer, Baltus. *The Hermit, or, An account of Francis Adam Joseph....* Mount Holly, NJ: Burlington County Herald, 1976.

Horan, Michael. *Index to Mount Holly (N.J.) Cemetery record of interments, 1840–1955.* New Jersey: M. Horan & J.M. Perinchief, 1981.

Humor and the Delaware Tribe, at www.delawaretribeofindians.nsn.us/humor.html, 2006.

Jackson, John W. *Margaret Morris: Her Journal with Biographical Sketch and Notes.* Philadelphia: George S. MacManus & Company, 1949.

King, William Harvey. *History of Homeopathy and its Institutions in America*, 2007. http://www.homeoint.org/history/king/4-12.htm.

Kozempel, Frank C. "The Camden and Burlington County Railway Company: The 125th Anniversary." *The High Line* 13 and 14 (Autumn/Winter 1993–1994).

Lane, Wheaton J. *From Indian Trail to Iron Horse: Travel and Transportation in New Jersey.* Princeton: Princeton University Press, 1939.

Losse, George. *A Historical Survey of the Ashurst Mansion.* Pemberton, NJ: Burlington County College, 1980.

McShulkis, Alicia. *Monograph* for Mount Holly Master Gardeners, 2007.

———. *Mount Holly Gardens*, The Big Berry, Fall, Main Street Mount Holly, 2005.

Mount Holly Cemetery Co. Mount Holly Cemetery records. Mount Holly, 1999.

Mount Holly Chamber of Commerce. *The Story of Mount Holly*. Mount Holly, NJ: Burlington County Library, 1960.

Mount Holly Herald. Historical and industrial edition, 1826–1916. Mount Holly, NJ: [s.n.], 1916.

Mount Holly Historical Society. Endowed postcard, photographic and family collections. Mount Holly, NJ.

Mount Holly Historical Society. Historic Archive Collection.

Mount Holly Library and Lyceum. Endowed post card, photographic and family collections, Mount Holly, NJ.

Mount Holly Methodist Church Records. *Marriages, baptisms (1833–1849, 1874–1918)*. Mount Holly: Burlington County Library, 1999.

New Jersey Mirror archives, 1814 to 1957. Westampton, NJ: Burlington County Library, 2007.

Newspaper extracts, 1775. Archives of the State of New Jersey, First Series, Vol. 31.

Nixon, Howard Gaskill. *The Life and Times of Howard Gaskill Nixon in and around Mount Holly, New Jersey*. Lumberton, NJ: H.G. Nixon, c1988.

Nusche, Jan. "Lying In." *Canadian Medical Association Journal* 167 (September 17, 2002).

Page, Jake. *In the Hands of the Great Spirit: The 20,000 Year History of American Indians*. New York: Free Press, 2003.

Parry, Edwin S. *Betsy Ross: Quaker Rebel*. Philadelphia: John Winston and Company, 1930.

Perinchief, Elizabeth Marren. *A History of St. Andrew's Church (Episcopal), 1742–1992*. Mount Holly: St. Andrew's Church, 1995.

———. *The Woolman family: Descendants of John Woolman and Elizabeth Borton, married 1684, who lived near Rancocas, Burlington County, New Jersey, included are descendants of John Woolman, Quaker preacher and journalist, through his daughter, Mary Woolman Comfort.* Mount Holly: John Woolman Memorial Association, 1991.

Read, Zachariah. "Dr. Zachariah Read's History of Mount Holly." Manuscript, 1859. Mount Holly Library and Lyceum Collection.

Recruiting of the British Army in the American Revolution, 2007. http://www.americanrevolution.org.

Rementer, Jim "Lenape Jim." "Pahsahn: The Lenape Indian Football Game." *Delaware Tribe of Indians* , 2006. www.delawaretribeofindians.nsn.us/football.html. Originally published in *Bulletin of the Archaeological Society of New Jersey* 48 (1993).

Reves, Haviland F. *A Reeves Genealogy: The Reeves Family, The Descendants of Walter Reeves of Burlington County, New Jersey, Through His Eldest Son, John*. Detroit, MI, 1930.

Shinn, Henry C. *The History of Mount Holly*. Mount Holly: Mount Holly Herald, 1957.

Smith, Mary L. "Facts Written by Mary Smith." Manuscript, Mount Holly Historical Society, 2004.

———. *Mount Holly Women Who Cared*. Mount Holly: Co-Works, Inc., and Mount Holly Historical Society, 1996.

———. "Taverns of Mount Holly." Manuscript, Mount Holly Historical Society, 1998.

Still, James. *Early Recollections and Life of Dr. James Still*. New Brunswick: Rutgers University Press, 1973.

Stock Market Crash Net. 2007. http://www.stock-market-crash.net/1929.htm

Stryker-Rodda, K. *Revolutionary Census of NJ, Hunterdon House*. Lambertville, NJ, 1986.

Town Meeting Minutes. Northampton, NJ: Census of Northampton, Burlington County, 1709.

Tustin, J. *The Widow of Mount Holly*. Woodbury, NJ: Gloucester County Historical Society Papers.

United States Army Training Center Infantry. *The History of Fort Dix, New Jersey, 1917–1967*. Fort Dix: Prepared by the Information Office, United States Army Training Center Infantry, 1967.

Von Donop, Col. Karl E. "Letter from Bordentown to General Howe in New York, December 1776." Stryker Revolutionary War Manuscript Collection, NJ Archives, Trenton, 2007.

Walker, Edwin Robert. *Proceedings of the New Jersey Historical Society, New Series* 2, no. 4 (1917).

Washington, George. Correspondence by Joseph Reed and Israel Putnam. George Washington Papers, Library of Congress, http://memory.loc.gov/ammem/gwhtml/gwhome.html

Wayne T. McCabe & Associates, Inc. *Historic Mount Holly Mill Race Revitalization Project: Historic Structure Report*. Newton, NJ: Wayne T. McCabe & Associates, Inc., 2005.

Weiss, Harry B. (Harry Bischoff) and Sim, Robert J., The Early Grist and Flouring Mills of New Jersey. Trenton : New Jersey Agricultural Society, 1956.

Weiss, H., and G. Weiss. *Forgotten Mills of New Jersey*. Trenton: New Jersey Agricultural Society, 1960.

Weiss, Harry B., and Grace M. Weiss. *Early Brick Making in New Jersey*. Trenton: New Jersey Agricultural Society, 1966.

Winzinger, Heidi J. Various interviews. Mount Holly Historical Society, 1998.

Winzinger, Heidi J., and Mary L. Smith. *Mount Holly*. Charleston, SC: Arcadia, 2001.

Woodward, E.M., and J.F. Hageman. *The History of Burlington & Mercer Counties With Biographical Sketches of Many of Their Pioneers and Prominent Men*. Philadelphia: Everts & Peck, 1883.

Woolman, John. *A Word of Remembrance and Caution to the Rich*. Burlington, NJ: S.C. Ustick, printer, 1803.

Wright, Giles R. *Afro-Americans in New Jersey*. New Jersey Historical Commission, Department of State, 1988.

Wright, Giles, and Edward Wonkeryor. *Steal Away, Steal Away: A Guide to the Underground Railroad in New Jersey*. Trenton: NJ Historical Commission, 2006.

Dennis C. Rizzo.